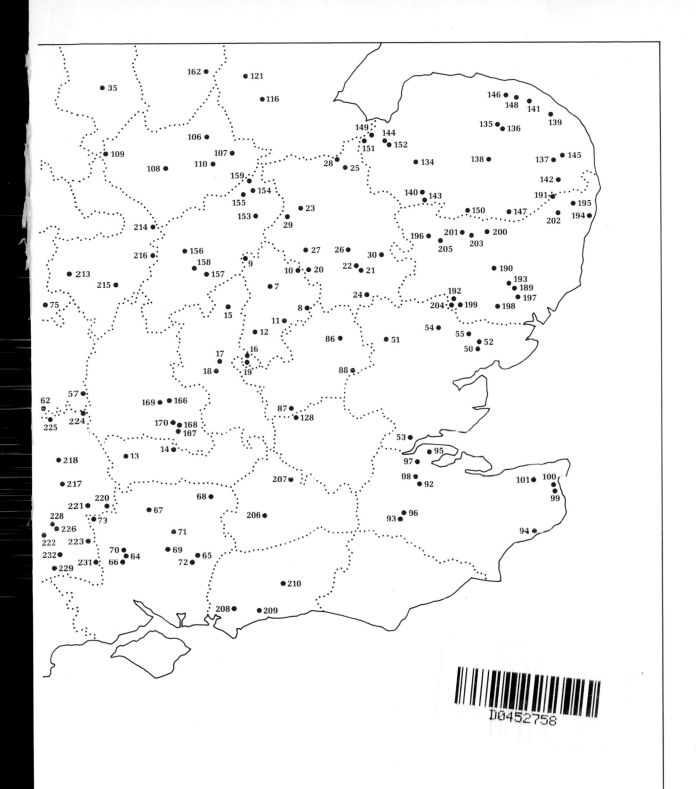

Distribution of churches in the care of the Fund before 31 March 1989: south.

A Victorian print of Paddlesworth.

REDUNDANT CHURCHES FUND

Churches in Retirement

A gazetteer

WITH FOREWORD BY J L CARR

'It is a reverend thing to see an ancient castle or
building not in decay' – FRANCIS BACON

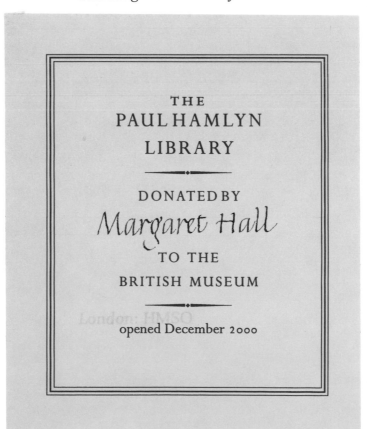

London: HMSO

© Copyright Controller of HMSO 1990
First published 1990
ISBN 0 11 701452 4

British Library Cataloguing in Publication Data

A CIP catalogue record for this book is available from the British Library

HMSO publications are available from:

HMSO Publications Centre
(Mail and telephone orders only)
PO Box 276. London. SW8 5DT
Telephone orders 071-873 9090
General enquiries 071-873 0011
(queuing system in operation for both numbers)

HMSO Bookshops
49 High Holborn, London. WC1V 6HB 071-873 0011 (Counter service only)
258 Broad Street, Birmingham. B1 2HE 021-643 3740
Southey House, 33 Wine Street. Bristol BS1 2BQ (0272) 264306
9–21 Princess Street, Manchester. M60 8AS 061-834 7201
80 Chichester Street, Belfast. BT1 4JY (0232) 238451
71 Lothian Road, Edinburgh. EH3 9AZ 031–228 4181

HMSO's Accredited Agents
(see Yellow Pages)

And through good booksellers

This book is intended to be an illustrated record of the 250 churches which were in the Fund's care in the Spring of 1989. It has three main purposes. First and foremost, it aims to encourage readers to visit the Fund's churches and to help them enjoy the experience. Secondly, it aims to increase public awareness of the implications of redundancy for the priceless church buildings of England and knowledge of what is being done to preserve them. Lastly, this book will serve as a memorial of the first 20 years of the Fund's existence and as a tribute to all who have contributed to its work.

GORDON BURRETT
Chairman
Redundant Churches Fund

Churches in Retirement is a tribute to the memory of Vivian Lipman, a Member of the Fund from 1979 until his death on 10 March 1990.

Contents

Foreword

We have seven Fund churches in Northamptonshire and, last week, I visited them. Their communities had shrunk, their futures had been doubtful. Now they were safe and in good trim: it was all very heartening.

Even twenty years ago, it might have been a more chastening journey. For it was only in 1969 that as a result of the Bridges Commission the Redundant Churches Fund was established. Even so, one of its earliest acquisitions was roofless. And elsewhere, dilapidation already had gone too far – at Faxton, for instance.

I first came across it in 1947. It was July and I was walking from Rugby across Northamptonshire to Sally's home in Essex. Meaning to pass the night in Broughton, I crossed from Lamport and struck out across fields towards Faxton. Well, its name was on my map, but the village had almost gone.

Of seven cottages sprinkled along grass tracks, four were collapsing and a fifth unoccupied. But smoke rose from chimneys of what may have been a manor house or rectory and there was the church, a low building with a two-bell turret. Inside, there were benches, a pulpit, a font, a hint of medieval paintings upon a flaking limewashed wall, and an enormous stovepipe slung across the single aisle. Almost every old church has its particular marvel: here, it was a marble monument high on the chancel wall – Sir Augustine Nicolls, a Jacobean judge at prayer.

Outside again, amongst sheep grazing between the headstones, Faxton brought to mind engravings in a Charles Dickens novel I had been reading, of Nell and her grandfather wandering through just such a scene in midland England. Another country, another age . . .

I didn't know at the time that, only a few years earlier, John Piper and the writer, Arnold Palmer, had passed that way, nor that they had reported: 'The timeworn, time-honoured church of St. Denys, one of the very few unrestored churches in these parts, needs no more than a certain amount of simple repairs if it is to be saved from the opposing dangers of decay and restoration . . .'. A few years later, in 1951, we came to live in the county. The big house had been abandoned and now only one woman, a Christmas-card designer, lived in Faxton. Whilst her husband was at sea, she had, as it were, pulled up the drawbridge and lived on her cottage's first floor, with a very small terrier for companion.

The little church was already under attack. Miss Joan Wake of Courteenhall (initiator of our County Record Office) wryly reported the efforts to prevent its destruction: 'All it achieved was a huge pile of correspondence.'

ix

When I visited a year later, the roof lead had been officially stripped and sold. The two bells lay cracked in a nettle patch beneath their turret. The furniture was smashed, the font and monument gone. Faxton Church was listed as 'an official organized ruin'.

More time passed. When Kettering Parish Church PCC was offered the Judge's monument, emissaries reported that this lay 'in hundreds of pieces on the floor of Lamport Rectory stable'. Doubtless this needed a second opinion but our financial nerve failed and we refused the gift. Someone said that Mr Cromwell of Great Doddington had rescued door jambs and a pillar and these were re-erected in his rectory garden. The 12th-century tub font had been installed in a 20th-century town church.

A year or two later, a local newspaper reported an appearance of 'the ghostly Faxton lady'. It was enough. Youths who had learnt enough geography to find the building but not enough history to spare it, moved in and demolition quickened. Commandos had nothing on this lot. Fires were lit on landings of the empty manor house, the Christmas-card lady's cottage was torn apart. There was a scatter of unearthed bones in the sanctuary. It truly is astonishing what can be done with boots and bare hands.

Miss Wake reported once more: 'Its category has been officially downgraded. Faxton Church has become "a dangerous structure." The ecclesiastical authorities have petitioned for its demolition.'

So the walls were flattened, the headstones buried face downward, the yard wall sagged to a grassy ridge. The late Sir Gyles Isham of Lamport Hall erected a stone plinth. Its simple inscription, 'the altar of the church of St Denys stood here', did not stir all hearts. When last I visited, this little column in an unkempt no man's land was wrapped in barbed wire, sole witness to a charming medieval church which had stood intact less than thirty years earlier.

Yet, although no more displayed on up-to-date maps, Faxton's name still jogs memories. The Judge's monument no longer marks his grave but, sheltered by a catalogue number, you can see it resurrected on a gallery wall in the Victoria and Albert Museum. And you may come across the four-volume *Recording England* (Oxford University Press, 1946), commissioned by the Pilgrim Trust – a collection of paintings and drawings of 'buildings of national importance particularly exposed to the danger of destruction in the operation of war'. In volume II you will find John Piper's drawing of the monument on Faxton's chancel wall and his painting of a doomed church alone in the fields.

But for the Fund there might have been scores of Faxtons and, amongst them, some of the buildings in this book. Nowadays, it is becoming rarer for churches and chapels in a really dire state to come the Fund's way and I am convinced that, in future years, with our continuing vigilance, what is rare now need never happen.

J L CARR
February 1989

Acknowledgements

The Fund is particularly indebted to two people. Christopher Dalton's photographs have for years been delightful and informative in the Fund's publications and in books, magazines and exhibitions elsewhere. Unless indicated otherwise the photographs are by him – it is in large part his book – and it is only appropriate that there are also pictures by two of his mentors, Edwin Smith and John Piper.

Michael Charlesworth undertook the task of establishing some coherence in the style of the many original contributors to the gazetteer. The Fund is deeply grateful for his editing and for the all too few examples of his wit that he permitted to appear.

Numbers below refer to gazetteer entries.

Penelope Adamson 206, Keith Barley 119, 246; Anthony Barnes 18, 140, Torbryan tower (introduction); Claude Blair 11; Mark Chatfield 33; Catherine Cullis, Little Barford (introduction); Michael Eastman 172; the Revd. Stuart Edwards 102; R M Friendship-Taylor 157; Neil Skelton 14, 82, 126, 182, 218, 222, 229; Philip Venning 184; Alec Vickerman 204; Kate Weaver 89, 211, 238, South Cowton (colour section); Geoffrey Wheeler 249.

Other pictures by courtesy of: the Bury Free Press, West Suffolk Newspapers Ltd. 203; Church Commissioners 54; F H Crossley, reproduced by permission of the Conway Librarian, Courtauld Institute of Art 15, 176; Doncaster Museum and Art Gallery 245; Essex County Council, Trustees of the Town Library, Saffron Walden Victorian Studies Centre 6, 58, 69, 71, 197, 243; F A Fowler, in Bedfordshire County Record Office 12; HTV West, Uphill (colour section); Norfolk Museums Service, Norwich Castle Museum 137, 151, Covehithe and Bungay (colour section), North Barningham (front cover); John Piper, photographs from the Tate Gallery 30, 171, and paintings by permission of Henry Thorold, Saltfleetby (colour section), and of R S Copestake, Theddlethorpe (colour section); Pitkin Pictorials Ltd., Chandos Mausoleum (colour section); Royal Commission on the Historical Monuments of England 2, 3, 32, 35, 37, 47, 50, 62, 68, 72, 73, 76, 78, 80, 84, 87, 92, 94, 95, 96, 107, 109, 121, 122, 132, 133, 139, 146, 158, 163, 173, 174, 178, 192, 193, 195, 220, 226, 228, 232, 234, 235, 236, 237, 247; the Royal Navy, by permission of the Photographic Section, HMS Osprey, Portland 44; Edwin Smith, by permission of Olive Cook 224, Didmarton (introduction), Cameley (back cover); by courtesy of the Board of Trustees of the Victoria and Albert Museum 1, 93, Paddlesworth (frontispiece); Wiltshire Archaeological and Natural History Society 225, Berwick Bassett (colour section).

Introduction

THE REDUNDANT CHURCHES FUND

PEOPLE

The Fund was established by law in 1969, following recommendations from a committee under Lord Bridges, with the charge of preserving, in the interests of the Nation and the Church of England, those churches of historical and archaeological interest or architectural quality which are no longer required for regular worship. Such churches pass into the ownership of the Fund which is financed by Church and State in partnership. By the end of 1989 some 260 churches had been vested in the Fund. Its annual expenditure was of the order of £2 million, of which 70 per cent was provided by the Department of the Environment and 30 per cent by the Church Commissioners. The Fund's responsibilities are confined to England.

To discharge this important and constantly expanding task the Fund has a board of trustees consisting of a Chairman and six members, and a permanent full-time staff of seven. The importance of the Fund's work and the need for it to be seen to be independent is underlined by the provision in the law that the Chairman and members should be appointed by Her Majesty The Queen, with the advice of the Archbishops of Canterbury and York submitted through the Prime Minister.

The Fund's job may be summarised as: the preservation of the churches vested in it as a unique and priceless part of the national heritage, having regard to their past as places of Christian worship and their continued existence as consecrated buildings. The aim is essentially to conserve and not to restore. The rule of thumb – which it is not always possible or desirable to observe rigidly – is to maintain a church broadly as it was when the last regular congregation went out of its doors, subject always to the requirements of economic repairs and maintenance. Changes wrought before redundancy, even if dubious to modern eyes, are normally to be retained as part of the history of the church. All this does not necessarily exclude, exceptionally, the restoration of previously hidden features, e.g., wall-paintings. In setting standards of repair and maintenance the Fund seeks to achieve the modest good order which might be the aim of a caring but not too wealthy parish.

The principal work of the Fund is therefore repair and maintenance. It is concerned essentially with bricks and mortar; with defeating decay and protection from the weather. If such a description of the Fund's central task seems to lack glamour the reality is, on the contrary, that the Fund has to deal with a very wide range of fascinating and often difficult problems. Within the unavoidable uncertainties of its five-year budgets, innumerable decisions have to be taken about work priorities, standards, the economy and architectural

Didmarton church.

1

acceptability of particular repairs, and general financial management. Judgments have to be made on architectural, antiquarian and aesthetic matters not only in relation to the church buildings but also to their contents and their churchyards. Local support and wider public interest must be encouraged. The local 'politics' often attaching to a redundant church must be sympathetically handled. Of crucial importance are the Fund's relationships with the 30–40 architects it employs to provide standing professional advice for each of its churches. These relationships must be made and kept as effective as possible.

Contrary to common belief, the Fund does not influence (or seek to influence) the selection of churches to be vested in it according to some estimate of its own about the strength of the case for their preservation. The decision to declare a church redundant is taken on pastoral grounds by the diocese concerned in consultation with the Church Commissioners. There follows a waiting period during which the diocese tries to find an acceptable alternative use for the church. If this search fails it is for the Church Commissioners to decide whether the church should be demolished or is of a quality to justify preservation by being vested in the Fund. In making their judgment the Church Commissioners are advised by another independent statutory body, the Advisory Board for Redundant Churches, which recommends whether, in its view, the church should be preserved. The Fund itself plays no part in this process other than to say whether it can meet the likely cost of repair. Once vested, all churches are cared for by the Fund with equal devotion. Within the limitations imposed by the statute, their occasional or temporary use is actively encouraged for both secular and religious purposes. The relinquishing of the Fund's churches for suitable alternative use also is permitted by its statute and positively encouraged in appropriate cases.

Members and Staff

The way one describes the work of the Fund depends upon the audience. In ecclesiastical terms the Fund may be compared with a diocese of 250 churches, such as Rochester. Any analogy as regards the administration is inadequate unless one were to liken the Fund members to a corporate episcopate, the staff to archdeacons, and the field officers to peripatetic rural deans! In business terminology the Fund members constitute a board of directors, with executives in the staff members servicing 250 outlets. But neither analogy is complete, for while the first indicates the extent of dedication found in Fund and members, the latter ignores the large numbers of key-holders and voluntary helpers.

In accordance with the Bridges Report, the Pastoral Measure was drawn up to provide that the Fund should be an independent body. It may receive money from both Church and State, but it is neither a State nor a Church body – it is independent. It is clear that the greatest care has been taken to ensure that the Fund members are experts in their own field and analysis will show that under each Chairman there have been people skilled, some in architecture and art history, from both Church and State backgrounds. There have been Parliamentarians, administrators, as well as those with an especial interest in the living church. While this has never been laid down, at least two of the members have been a layman and a clergyman from the General Synod, so a link with the Church of England has been strongly maintained.

Members of the Fund, staff and local supporters at Little Barford.

While the Chairman is not responsible for the appointment of members of the Fund, it will be easiest to describe them under the chairmanship of the three Chairmen (not that the whole Fund membership changed at the inception of a chairmanship, as several members in each case overlapped from one period to the next).

Ivor Bulmer-Thomas (Chairman 1969–76) came from a distinguished career in Parliament and is a deeply dedicated lifelong preserver of our ancient heritage, having personally founded the Friends of Friendless Churches. As first Chairman he moulded the policy of the Fund, eagerly concerned to save churches, and ensuring that they were obviously to be seen as buildings still consecrated to the worship of Almighty God. Thanks to him the Fund's first home was, and remains, the Church of St Andrew-by-the-Wardrobe, of which he is a churchwarden. For many years the Fund met in the dining-room of the Rectory of St Andrew's.

Details of those gathered around him follow. Lord Anglesey (member, 1969–78) of Plas Newydd, is a distinguished historian and author. E S Bishop (member, 1969–74), later Lord Bishopton, was MP for Newark and resigned after becoming Second Churches' Estate Commissioner. R P T Gibson (member, 1969–71), later Lord Gibson, resigned when he became Chairman of the Arts Council, having formerly been Chairman of the National Trust. Dean J W A Hussey of Chichester (member, 1969–77) applied to the work of the Fund the artistic flair with which he enhanced his Cathedral. Paul Paget (member, 1969–76) of the firm of Seely and Paget brought the same exemplary taste to redundant churches as he did to other buildings in his care. Sir Edward Muir (member, 1969–76) had a distinguished career in the Ministry of Works, being Permanent Secretary 1962–5 and combined chairmanship of the Ancient Monuments Board (1966–78) with membership of the Fund. John L E (now Sir

John) Smith (member, 1972–4), who was the founder of the Landmark Trust, and Sir Gilbert Inglefield (member 1974–6), who was Lord Mayor of London (1967–8), a Church Commissioner (1962–78), and a Royal Fine Arts Commissioner (1968–75), also made considerable contributions in the early days of the Fund.

Firm foundations laid by the first Chairman and members were built upon by their successors. Sir David Stephens (Chairman, 1976–81) brought experience from his career of public service, including the Clerkship of the Parliaments, to the administration of the Fund. During his chairmanship, Dean Henry Stapleton (member since 1976), contributed his historical, ecclesiological and pastoral interests.

Corinne Bennett (member, 1976–9) provided much necessary advice in the technical and architectural fields. Her place was later to be taken by Alan Rome (member since 1980) architect to among other places, Salisbury Cathedral and Lancing College Chapel. Dr Vivian Lipman (member since 1979) had served as Director of Ancient Monuments and Historic Buildings in the Department of the Environment, and is an historian, specialising in Jewish history. Major Gerald Charrington (member since 1977), a former member of the General Synod, has practical experience of the care of historic parish buildings and is an historic house owner. Lord Kennet (member, 1978–80), joint author of a book on London churches, provided valuable awareness of the need for accountability in the expenditure of public funds; he resigned his appointment when he became SDP Defence Spokesman in the House of Lords in 1980. Archdeacon Norman McDermid (member, 1977–89) provided sensitivity and awareness of pastoral needs, frequently acting as an interpreter of the Fund's purpose to Synod members.

As Sir David's successor, Gordon Burrett (Chairman since 1982) was appointed and has provided useful knowledge of 'how things work' based on his experience in the Diplomatic Service, the Treasury, the Cabinet Office and the former Civil Service Department. Claude Blair (member since 1982), the distinguished art historian, former Keeper of Metalwork at the Victoria & Albert Museum, and a member of the Council for the Care of Churches' Executive Committee, has detailed knowledge of the contents which survive in so many of our churches.

The Fund is an organism. Not only does its work grow but its spirit is nurtured by a devoted group of staff. There can be few bodies – the choice of the word is deliberate – which have enjoyed such loyalty and devotion. Of the headquarters staff, John Bowles has been Secretary since the Fund's inception and his knowledge of precedents and buildings is unsurpassed. Desmond Ward came from the Church Commissioners as Director (1979–84), serving the Fund with wit and wisdom after his long career at Millbank. In 1984 Anthony Barnes became Director with a different portfolio and has done much to advance the image of the Fund in publicity and publication. Jean Southon (Assistant Secretary 1975–8) was inventive in ways of making redundant churches 'live'. Catherine Cullis, who succeeded her, provides valuable architectural knowledge and ensures that relationships with the local people are good. Of our field officers, Christopher Dalton (staff since 1976) has surveyed the churches with

4

ladder and camera. He is an expert on church bells and the high standard of his photography is everywhere commended. Neil Skelton (staff since 1980) has similar interests, combined with the churchwardenship of a busy town church. Kate Weaver (staff since 1988) with an architectural background, is responsible for the East Anglian group of churches. Supporting both Fund members and staff, there has been a remarkable succession of secretarial assistants: Olive Catherine (1970–74), Adelaide Millard (1977–9), Marjory McLaren (1979–83) and Margaret Kiely (since 1983). The Fund owes its profound thanks to them for all the work they have done, and do, so well.

Such a description of the members of the Fund is inadequate to describe its spirit. It has its own ethos, particular to itself. As one member has put it, it is a favourite committee, with all the members and staff united in a single aim, each in turn making their own contribution.

Re-rendering Torbryan tower.

Mr Bernard Jeffs, stonemason, on scaffolding at Deene.

Architects, Craftsmen and Local Helpers

As mentioned, the Fund's aim is to repair and maintain its buildings to the standard that might be aimed at by a caring but not especially wealthy congregation – in the words of William Morris, 'to put Protection in the place of Restoration' and 'to resist all tamperings with either the fabric or ornament of the building as it stands'. It also tries to leave its buildings unlocked or accessible through local key-holders, and aims to provide guidebooks or equivalent information, but stopping short of the full documentation one would expect in a museum.

Clearly all this cannot be achieved for 250 churches by a full-time staff of seven and a small group of part-timers. Throughout the country the Fund has enlisted helpers who clean its churches, report defects or damage, provide flowers, change altar frontals and generally care for the building. It is they who give the churches the sense of life that they usually have.

In many places committees of Friends have been formed who keep the church and, sometimes, the Fund up to the mark. It is they who generate ideas about exhibitions, concerts and other events that would be suitable and would enable the building to recover a role in its community. Only local knowledge can do this well.

Wherever possible churches are left open. Where this cannot be risked a notice will tell you where to find the key-holder – and if vandals have removed or election posters obscured this notice please tell us.

Repairs and maintenance are carried out by a network of architects and contractors who specialise in the conservation of old buildings. The Fund has chosen not to employ a staff of architects but to make use of the services, on contract, of architects specialising in the care of cathedrals, abbeys and college chapels who prepare the quinquennial reports on parish churches and carry out the repairs recommended in them. Many of the architects who work for the Fund were once scholars of the Society for the Protection of Ancient Buildings. They provide a pool of expertise that is, fortunately, reasonably distributed geographically.

As with architects so with contractors, but the distribution of the latter is much more uneven. Some jobs are so large that only a few firms, significant regionally if not nationally, can tackle them with sufficient competence in all departments. In some areas the only contractor the Fund can count upon goes helter-skelter from one church to another – often a two or three man team, aided in one case by a dog. Wherever possible, the Fund seeks contractors with local knowledge and an ability with local materials. It is very noticeable that many younger people are now committing themselves to this work, despite its anonymity. One visitor, to Shorncote, could hardly believe that the whole roof had been retiled, so well did it convey a sense of its age. The young builders who heard her were delighted.

The Fund also employs specialist conservators who look after wall-paintings, monuments, stained glass, brasses, organs, bells and other artefacts. Beyond all these people are innumerable and generous advisers and friends: archaeologists, employees of English Heritage and the National Trust, diocesan staff and clergy and many others. The Fund tries to be as available to them as they are to the Fund.

BUILDINGS

A Microcosm of English Church Architecture

The 250 churches recorded in this book show that the Fund is, in practice, running an unique and widely dispersed repository of English ecclesiastical architecture.

The best example of Saxon work is the tower at Bywell. There is Norman work in many buildings – Edlington, Normanby and Thurlbear are three good examples, with work of considerable sophistication at Hales, Tortington and Wakerley. Shrewsbury has fine quality work from this and most subsequent periods.

All kinds of Gothic are to be found, at its grandest at Conington, Edlesborough, Gloucester, Hockwold, Torbryan, the Lichfield chapel at Evesham and the bell tower at West Walton. In a way, though, it is the sudden moment of eloquence that is most exciting: the east window at Haltham-on-Bain, the roof at Stretford, the medieval faces or beasts at Aldwincle, Idmiston and Parson Drove, the light and space at Wolfhampcote. Often, however, it is the *tout ensemble* which moves, the medieval church which has survived restoration and refurnishing, Eastleach, Haceby, Icklingham, Lower Gravenhurst, Sapiston, Shimpling, Theddlethorpe or Whenby. In all of these a spirituality has survived the Reformation and many subsequent fashions, even redundancy – a reminder that in tampering with these buildings one is dealing with something very old, very profound, a part of a precious folk culture. Classification is artificial, for the great value of so many of these buildings is as examples of the accretions of history: Old Dilton is medieval with a mass of later box-pews or other furnishings. The Fund is fortunate in having many of these churches that have grown like Topsy in its care. York's Holy Trinity Goodramgate is the most famous and most visited. St John on the Wall at Bristol is remarkable also for its situation atop the city wall. Inglesham is another, Saxon in origin and with wall-paintings of various dates emerging from the limewash on almost every wall. For many Badley is the most moving, one of the Fund's pilgrimage churches with the pale grey furnishings, a reward for the bumpy ride down the lane to the church. Cameley spans nearly as many centuries as Inglesham. Others of this kind are to be found at Little Washbourne, Parracombe, Stanstead Abbotts and Winterborne Tomson.

The 17th century was not a busy time for church building but the Fund has a number of good examples in its care: Oxhey Chapel of 1612; St John's Briggate in Leeds from the 1630s; the strongly Protestant chapel at Guyhirn, built as the monarchy was being restored in 1660. A rare country church from the end of the century is the charming Billesley of 1692. To these one might add Lady Anne Clifford's rebuilding of Brougham, also 1660.

The 18th century was, on the contrary, a great time for building as well as refurnishing. The style continued until the revolution of the Oxford Movement. The Fund has many churches associated with large estates, big municipal churches and humbler buildings for parochial use. The estate churches often were medieval, such as Spetchley, but came to assume an 18th-century character, as at Withcote. Gothick is to be seen in the sad shell of Henry Keene's Hartwell (1753–56) and at Croome D'Abitot. At the end of the period is Smirke's Mausoleum for the Duke of Newcastle at Milton. But for sheer visual excitement the best must be that first glimpse of Robert Adam's Gunton, preferably through nearly leafless trees in November.

There are fine municipal churches – often with a mayor's pew or other insignia of office – at Sunderland, Worcester, Lancaster, Bristol St Thomas and Macclesfield. Portland is as formal, with its echo of St Paul's and its two pulpits. At Chichester the pulpit stands in front of the altar. This supremacy of the Word is echoed in the seating of Skelton and Fylingdales. There are simpler, more vernacular churches, as at Tarleton and Pilling, where the erecting of Victorian buildings left the old church unaltered. A late example of the Common Prayer style is at Sutton Mallet, 1827–9. There then followed the

Oxford Movement and a frenzy of building and restoration equal to that which had taken place in the 15th century.

The Fund has many examples of work both by the famous Victorian architects and by some of the less well-known, as well as excellent restorations (by Blomfield at Little Barford, Pearson at Burley and Pountney Smith at Battlefield among the best). Bodley at Cambridge, Pearson at Chute Forest, Arthur Blomfield at Privett, Pugin and Hardman assisting Daukes at Tetbury, are among the great names; Elwin at Booton, Conybeare at Itchen Stoke, Johnson of Alexandra Palace fame at South Tidworth, and Moore and Freer at Yazor all designed excellent buildings. In the north the Fund has an Edmund Sharpe church at Blackburn, and a Paley and Austin at Bolton.

Inevitably an account of this kind can read like a catalogue and, also, it can be so architecturally oriented that it forgets the purpose for which the buildings were first constructed. Luckily the public does not – both the people in the neighbourhood, who go enthusiastically to the few services; also the wider public, who come in to meditate or pray, most notably at Cambridge St Peter and at Whitcombe. We hope this book will encourage such people to discover Birdforth, Coston, Kingerby and many others.

FURNISHINGS

Because of the arbitrary nature of the way Fund churches are selected the church furnishings cannot be arranged into coherent patterns, art-historically, typologically, or even regionally, for a survey like this. All that can be done is to draw attention to some of the more interesting items in the different categories represented.

Bells

A number of churches have interesting rings of bells, as for example at Thurlbear and Torbryan (two complete pre-Reformation rings of four), Chadshunt (a 17th-century ring of six), Elworthy, Croome D'Abitot, Gloucester and Worcester. At Redbourne and Swaffham Prior are two virtually untouched 18th-century rings. Some individual bells are of outstanding importance. Bywell, Warminghurst and Wormsley have examples from the early 13th century and one of c.1300 from Hales is now in the King's Lynn Museum. Amongst places where other medieval bells remain are: Colemore (c.1380, cast at the Wokingham foundry), Wolfhampcote (c.1450 by John Sturdy of London), Chickney (two of c.1460–80 by John Kebyll), South Somercotes (two of 1423, beautifully inscribed and probably cast at Lincoln), Covehithe and Sudbury. Hockwold, St. Peter's, Cambridge, Cooling, Pensford and Stanton retain notable oak bell-frames of the 14th and 15th centuries. Amongst later bells the work of the Rudhalls of Gloucester is inevitably well represented, for example at Macclesfield and Croome D'Abitot, while the latter place has also four bells of 1651–62 by John Martin of Worcester. Mention should also be made of the Laudian bell of 1627 at Colemore, by Ellis Knight of Reading.

Fonts

Outstanding is one of the rare English Romanesque lead fonts, from Barnetby-le-Wold, but now lent to local museums in turn. Decorated with leaf motifs, it dates from c.1170. Fine stone fonts of the same period are at Pitstone, (Aylesbury type with arcading), and St Peter's, Cambridge. The latter is formed of figures of mermen, carved in the round, holding the tips of their forked tails. Amongst the many late-Gothic fonts of conventional form are those at Chickney, (with coats-of-arms); Clixby, (with figures of saints and rosettes; originally from Low Toynton); South Somercotes, (with the Instruments of the Passion); and Hales, (supported on eight angels standing on lions). The only post-Reformation fonts that call for special mention are the beautiful wooden one at Croome D'Abitot, carved with foliage and cherubs' heads, and attributed to Robert Adam; at Oxhey, and the Norman Shaw font at St John's, Leeds. The best font covers are at Wiggenhall (1625) and Nuneham Courtenay (Italian baroque).

Glass

Very many of the Fund's churches contain early glass, mostly too fragmentary to make much sense, though some, like Edworth, Elworthy, and Kirk Sandall, contain fine complete panels. The major holdings, however, are in three churches. Firstly, St Mary's, Shrewsbury, contains a large collection of magnificent glass, though none of it was actually made for the church. It includes an English Jesse window datable to 1327–53, and 15th- and early-16th-century glass from Germany and the Low Countries, amongst it some panels from the abbeys of Herchenrode and Altenberg. Those from the latter place are described by Pevsner as 'amongst the most valuable and most completely preserved German glass of their date'. Secondly, Holy Trinity, Goodramgate, York, where, amongst other locally-produced late-medieval glass, the splendid east window of 1470–1, presented by the priest John Walker, is famous. Thirdly, the windows of Withcote Chapel are almost entirely filled with glass of c.1530–40 which has been attributed to King Henry VIII's glazier, Galeon Hone, whose work at King's College Chapel it resembles stylistically.

Interesting 18th-century glass by William Peckitt of York is at Allerton Mauleverer, while many of the famous 19th-century stained-glass craftsmen and designers are well represented in the Fund's churches: William Morris (All Saints, Cambridge); Hardman & Co (St Peter's, Sudbury, and St John's, Leeds); C E Kempe (Saundby, Little Barford, and Colemore); William Collins (Redbourne) and William Wailes (Albury); Clayton and Bell (Burley-on-the-Hill, Cooling, Hockwold, Ozleworth); Westlake & Co (Burley-on-the-Hill); Willement (Tortington and Evesham); F C Eden (Kedleston).

Monuments and other sculpture

This category contains more major pieces than any other, for the obvious reason that the objects included in it are the least moveable of all furnishings. There are very few churches that do not have a memorial of some kind, while those at, for example, Harewood, Croome d'Abitot, Deene, Kedleston, and Little Stanmore, (the Chandos Mausoleum) are major repositories.

Sculptured stone and wood
A few churches contain fragments of pre-Conquest carvings, amongst them some 'Viking' stones at Preston Deanery, portions of crosses at Bywell and Wroxeter, a grave slab at St Mary's, Shrewsbury, a 'stone' at Coverham, and a Madonna and Child at Inglesham – all Anglo-Saxon. A Romanesque tympanum at Billesley is an important example of the 12th-century Herefordshire school of sculpture, while capitals at Wakerley are decorated with remarkable carvings of the same period. High-quality sculptured panels reputedly from Haughmond Abbey, now much defaced but apparently of the 13th century, are set in a frieze round the top of the tower at Wroxeter.

Monumental sculpture
This begins with a group of characteristic 13th- and 14th-century North-Country cross-slabs, many bearing symbols of the avocations of the people commemorated, for example at Bywell and, a beautifully-carved specimen, at Throapham. The earliest effigies in the round are the early 14th-century freestone knight at St Mary's, Shrewsbury, and the beautiful and sensitive Purbeck-marble figure of *c.*1330 at Conington which, uniquely, shows a knight with his armour covered by a Franciscan robe. Contemporary with these are the rare wooden knights at Allerton Mauleverer, and the partly-buried cross-slab at Kedleston, with the bas-relief heads of a knight and lady in quatrefoils. Later 14th-century effigies of note, all freestone, are the high-quality, though muti-lated, Westminster-school knight of *c.*1330–40 at St Peter's, Sandwich, the two knights and ladies at Stretford, and the knight on his original tomb at Buslingthorpe – all of which date from *c.*1340–50 – and the Bristol-school figure of a merchant, *c.*1388, in St John the Baptist, Bristol. Other interesting 14th-century freestone effigies are at Kingerby (two knights and a civilian). In the field of pre-Reformation monuments, the greatest strength of the Fund lies in the major alabaster effigial tombs under its care, all dating from the early 15th century onwards. One of the largest collections in any one church in Britain is at Harewood, while other examples are at Kedleston, South Cowton, East Shefford, Chilton, and Deene. The alabaster tombs were produced in the same Derbyshire and York workshops as the carved panels (tables) that were England's one internationally-known medieval art export, and these are represented by 15th-century examples in St Mary's, Shrewsbury. One other contemporary example of non-monumental sculpture that must be mentioned because of its great rarity in this country, though it is much decayed, is the wooden *pietà* at Battlefield.

Post-Reformation memorials are, of course, legion, and range in style from the simple churchyard gravestone of an 18th-century village blacksmith, carved with the tools of his trade and an appropriate epitaph, at Shotley, to Bertram Mackennal's sumptuous marble tomb, with effigies, of Marquess Curzon of Kedleston (d. 1925) and his wife. Between these two extremes, almost all forms of monument are to be found in the Fund's churches. The pomposity, often over heavy, of the Elizabethan and early-Jacobean periods is well represented at Wroxeter, St Nicholas's, Gloucester; Moulton, North Barningham, West Dean, Freefolk, and Croome D'Abitot. One of the monuments in the last church is probably by Nicholas Stone, who is also represented at Blatherwycke. Later 17th-century monuments of note are at: All Saints, Conington, including one attributed to Grinling Gibbons, who also carved another monument at Croome D'Abitot; Hardington Bampfylde, perhaps by William Stanton; Kedleston, and

12th-century Agnus Dei at Duxford.

West Dean, attributed to John Bushnell. Outstanding amongst the numerous 18th-century monuments are those to the Countess of Richmond (d. 1722), at Deene, and Sir Nathaniel Curzon (d. 1758), at Kedleston – the former by G B Guelfi, and the latter by J M Rysbrack after a design by Robert Adam. Other memorials of the period worthy of mention are those by Robert Singleton and other East Anglian sculptors at Hockwold, the earliest known monument by Robert Taylor, at Chadshunt, the Berkeley monuments at Spetchley and the

Screen at Torbryan.

11

extraordinary Hopper Mausoleum at Shotley. The continuing neo-Classical style of the 19th century is represented by the work of R W Sievier at Deene, Sir Francis Chantrey at Burley-on-the-Hill, Sir Richard Westmacott in the Milton Mausoleum, and St Mary's, Shrewsbury; and Robert Dunbar of Carlisle at Sunderland. For the later 19th century, the memorial at Esher to Princess Charlotte and her husband, commissioned by Queen Victoria from the local sculptor F J Williamson, is of interest because of its associations. The masterpiece of Victorian sculpture in the Fund's care, however, is at Deene: J E Boehm's superb monument to the 7th Earl of Cardigan – who led the charge of the Light Brigade – and his wife, with double effigies which reveal the characters of the noble pair with unflattering accuracy! The one major 20th-century monument, at Kedleston, has already been mentioned.

Brasses and associated items
Amongst the few incised slabs, the 15th-century ones at East Horndon, Redbourne, Stretton-en-le-Field, Shrewsbury, and Holdenby, are of note. Good monumental brasses, on the other hand, are numerous. The most important are two of the earliest brasses to survive anywhere. These are the small London-made figure of a lady of *c.*1310–25 at Pitstone, and the famous demi-figure of Sir Richard de Buslingthorpe at Buslingthorpe, which dates from *c.*1330, and was perhaps produced in Lincoln. Also outstanding is the magnificent Flemish brass to Thomas Pounder (1525) from St Mary Quay, Ipswich, now shown in Christchurch Mansion museum there. Other brasses of interest are at Adderley (late 14th-century abbot or bishop); Allerton Mauleverer (York school knight and lady, 1400); Albury (knight, 1440); Brougham (to Lord Brougham and Vaux, d. 1868, and his mother); Coverham (18th-century engraved plates in the churchyard); Cowthorpe (Baron of the Exchequer and lady holding a church, 1494, now mutilated); Little Wenham (knight and lady, 1514); North Barningham (knight and lady, 1516); East Shefford (knight and lady, 1524); West Harling (priest, 1479, two knights and ladies, *c.*1490 and 1508).

Finally, there are cast-iron gravestones at Bridgnorth and East Peckham.

Paintings
This category is represented in the Fund's churches mainly by wall-paintings, hatchments, royal arms and the occasional painted screen, though there also are a few painted altar-pieces, as well as one or two detached paintings in frames. Amongst the last, mention need only be made of the painting of Christ and the two Marys by Sebastiano Ricci, at Walpole, now on loan to the Fitzwilliam Museum, Cambridge, and the portrait by Thomas Wright of Derby of Charles Roe, the founder of Christ Church, Macclesfield.

Perhaps the greatest conservation problem that the Fund has to face is that of wall-paintings, which have the habit of turning up unexpectedly during the course of other work in a church. When they do, they are frequently not only in need of urgent – and immensely expensive – treatment, but if, as is often the case, they are superimposed in layers, they also present peculiarly difficult technical and philosophical problems about the way in which the treatment is to be carried out. Examples of this are provided by the major collections of medieval and later wall-paintings at Duxford and Inglesham – where these problems are compounded by damp and unstable wall-conditions – and at East

Shefford. Other important medieval wall-paintings are at Capel (13th century), Hales, (13th-15th century); Little Wenham, Moulton, Tarrant Crawford, and Broughton (14th century), and Albury (15th century).

Post-Reformation wall-paintings, of which there are many examples, are confined to ornamental designs, often incorporating texts. Outstanding are the 19th-century stencilled decorative schemes in A W Pugin's Drummond Chapel at Albury (by T Earley), Bodley's All Saints, Cambridge (by William Morris and F R Leach), and the extraordinary heraldic panels on the ceiling of Holy Trinity, Blackburn.

Woodwork

Woodwork is, of course, almost as plentiful in the Fund's churches as are monuments, but the number of outstanding examples is much smaller. The best medieval screens are at Torbryan, East Ruston, Wiggenhall and Little Barford, where they are embellished with painting. Theddlethorpe, Saltfleetby, Inglesham and Kirk Sandall are of considerable interest, as is Chilton which is actually documented. Good medieval bench-ends are at Thurgarton, and Wordwell, but the outstanding set is at Wiggenhall St Mary the Virgin. Fine doors remain at Charfield and Higham. The outstanding medieval pieces, however, are the 'Easter Sepulchre' – a remarkable survival – at Cowthorpe, and the iron-mounted chest at Icklingham, mentioned under *Miscellaneous* below. Amongst a number of other chests, that at Pitstone should be mentioned.

The most important 16th-century piece is the superb Renaissance screen at Holdenby, originally made for the great house built there by Sir Christopher Hatton, Lord Chancellor and Elizabeth I's favourite. The Fund's supreme single collection of woodwork, however, is in the astonishing Gothic-survival church of St John, Leeds (consecrated in 1634), which, with its towering Royal Arms over the screen, produces an unforgettable effect, despite extensive restoration. Comparable, though less impressive, is the screen at Adderley. Less sophisticated, but the more enchanting in consequence, are the churches that retain their simple 18th- or early 19th-century wood furnishings, box-pews, two- and three-decker pulpits and the rest, virtually unchanged. Notable examples are at Parracombe (where the unusual tympanum above the screen is known to have been cleaned in 1758), Little Washbourne, Chiselhampton, Old Dilton, Inglesham, Skelton and Fylingdales, while at Haltham-on-Bain, medieval and 17th-century woodwork has been reassembled and supplemented to produce a remarkable 18th-century ensemble. There are a number of fine Jacobean pulpits, for example at Moreton Jeffries, and the Gothick pulpit, attributed to Robert Adam, at Croome D'Abitot in the same county is outstanding. Finally, a curious survival, at Wiggenhall, is a ladder dated 1694.

Miscellaneous

The Fund's churches contain many types of objects which do not lend themselves to separate categorization because the number of examples worth mentioning in a survey of this kind is too small. They include numerous funerary hatchments, Royal Arms, organs, turret-clocks, tiles and metalwork of all kinds, as well as such great rarities as the maidens' garlands at Fylingdales, the 15th-century embroidered pall and 17th-century altar-cloth from St Peter's, Sudbury, now kept in the Ipswich Museum, and the medieval shrine at Stretford.

Amongst organs, of special importance is the one at Brownsover, because of its carved case of *c*.1668 from St John's College, Cambridge and the "west-country" style case of 1728 by John Harris at St Thomas the Martyr, Bristol. Outstanding as musical instruments are those of St Swithun, Worcester (*c*.1780, builder unknown, a remarkable survival for the quantity and quality of original 18th-century pipework and its early console); Bolton (1882 by Isaac Abbott, unaltered) and Shrewsbury (1912 unaltered, by J J Binns) behind one of the best surviving early 18th-century cases – Harris and Byfield, 1724.

17th-century turret-clocks are at Esher and Burley-on-the-Hill, the latter of special interest in that it is signed by the great London clockmaker Joseph Knibb and dated 1678.

The late-medieval latten eagle lectern at Wiggenhall is remarkable. An outstanding example of the art of the blacksmith is provided by the wrought-iron mounts on the 14th-century chest from All Saints, Icklingham, now in neighbouring St James's. Equally remarkable in its own way is the Hardman corona lucis gasolier of 1848, presumably designed by A W Pugin, at Tetbury, a church that also contains other interesting fittings for gaslights of the same period. Noteworthy too are the gates designed by Robert Adam and Norman Shaw respectively at Croome D'Abitot, and St John's, Leeds, and the early 20th-century iron screen round Marquess Curzon's chapel at Kedleston. Good medieval encaustic tiles are at All Saints, Icklingham, and Pitstone, and fine 19th-century ones in Pugin's Drummond Chapel at Albury, and (by Minton) at All Saints, Cambridge. St John's, Leeds, contains a striking 19th-century mosaic reredos by Salviati of Venice.

Some communion plate of importance has been vested in the Fund, but it is never displayed in its churches, for security reasons, as likewise, amongst the few pieces of church armour, the important 15th-century helmet from East Shefford, which has for many years been on loan to the Royal Armouries in the Tower of London.

Gazetteer of Churches in the Care of the Redundant Churches Fund

AVON

1 Bristol, St John on the Wall
ST 587 732

The site is at least as early as the 12th century and St John's is actually a part of the old city wall, the crypt being within it and the church's proportions limited by it. The tower and spire stand above one of the original gates.

The present church is late 14th-century and was founded by Walter Frampton (d. 1388), three times Mayor of Bristol, whose tomb is in the north wall. Most of the furnishings are 17th-century, presenting the look of a church of those years, relatively little altered since George Whit-field is said to have preached his first sermon from this pulpit. The Frampton tomb, Rowley brass and other furnishings convey the impression of a prosperous merchants' church in an enlightened age.

Below is the 14th-century vaulted crypt, earlier than the church, at least at its east end, containing two recumbent effigies. This is all medieval mystery, as in the picture by Samuel Prout, despite the confident commercial faith above. To the east is a conduit forming part of the city's medieval water supply.

2 Bristol, St Thomas the Martyr
ST 591 727

A fine classical building of 1792–93, this church was designed by James Allen, a noted Bristol architect. This is no provincial attempt to mimic London. St Thomas's stands in its own right with, as Peter Burman has remarked, something of the style and impact of a church in Rome, for the handsome east end is in a busy commercial street. From here one goes into a small courtyard and then into the cool and spacious church.

As at Winsford, James Allen's design retains the 15th-century west tower of the earlier church. There is a fine ring of eight bells, all cast by local founders from the 15th to the 19th century. At the east end is a reredos of 1716 and at the west a gallery of 1728–32, both transferred from the previous church. On the north of the chancel is a superb 18th-century organ case.

Some of the other furnishings are 18th-century but most date from the 1896 res-

toration by H Roumieu Gough. They are excellently designed and all contribute to one of the best interiors in Bristol.

3 Cameley, St James
ST 610 576

One of a number of Fund churches which were particular favourites with John Betjeman, it lies in the valley of the River Cam, less than a mile west of Temple Cloud, which is equidistant from Bristol and Wells on the A47.

The church is of 11th-century foundation, largely rebuilt in the 15th century. It consists of nave, with south porch added in the 15th century, chancel and tower, the last being built of warm Mendip stone in contrast to the local limestone (blue lias) of the nave and chancel. An unusual feature is the external stone staircase west of the porch which gives access to the galleries.

The interior is a delightful mixture of periods and textures. The chancel arch and south doorway date from the 12th century, the latter having a bold interlacing rope motif. There are medieval and Georgian pews, a west gallery of 1711 and a south gallery dating from 1819. In the north-east corner of the nave stand the early 17th-century pulpit, with its octagonal tester, and the clerk's and rectory pews. Repairs during this century have revealed successive layers of wallpaintings, the earliest probably as old as the building itself, and showing traces of masonry patterns. There is much more, including a fine St Christopher and a delightfully framed set of Commandments above the chancel arch.

4 Charfield, St James
ST 719 912

The church lies on a steep hillside, not quite overlooking the present Charfield in its valley, three miles east of the M5 motorway. It was rebuilt in the early 15th century on the plan of a 12th-century structure.

The removal of ivy has revealed a pretty saddleback tower. The roofs are of Cotswold stone and the large windows flood the church with light. The door is particularly fine and the porch is noteworthy, with corner buttresses, pierced parapets and a contemporary inscription.

5 Pensford, St Thomas à Becket Tower
ST 618 637

Six miles south of Bristol, dramatically set against the sixteen arches of the now disused railway viaduct of 1873, the 14th-century west tower of this church has been transferred to the Fund.

Built of local rubble, it has three stages, with diagonal buttresses and a squat pyramidal roof. The west doorway has a finely moulded arch, while the rather unusual windows of the top stage are probably 15th-century.

Inside, the tower has an elaborate tierceron vault supported in three corners by wall shafts and in the fourth by a corbel head. Above it is a magnificent medieval bell-frame. A Perpendicular font, an early 17th-century hexagonal pulpit, benefaction board of 1797 and 19th-century Lord's Prayer and Decalogue, are all within the tower.

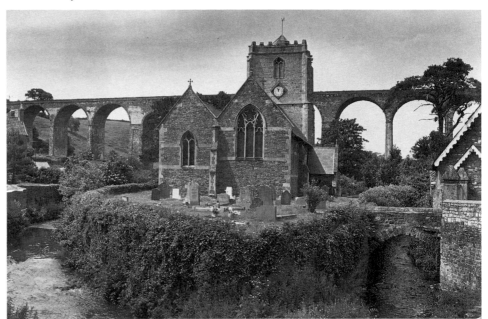

The nave has subsequently been unroofed.

6 Uphill, St Nicholas
ST 316 584

Built on a hill above the Roman port of Axium, St Nicholas feels as if it is more in sympathy with its past than with Weston-Super-Mare, which spreads northwards along the shore. It is a Norman church with central tower, chancel, unroofed nave and a north porch sheltering a Norman doorway. The stiff climb up to the church is amply rewarded, not least by the view in all directions.

BEDFORDSHIRE

7 Bedford, St Mary
TL 051 494

St Mary's was the first church to be built in Bedford on the south side of the River Ouse, and its distinctive early-Norman central tower and transepts are a prominent feature of the townscape and familiar landmarks to the railway traveller on both routes to Bedford.

The setting of the church is dominated by traffic but picturesque, and the small churchyard is full of trees and shrubs with many good 18th-century headstones. To the north and east it is surrounded mainly by pre-Victorian houses; indeed the immediate area to the north has changed little since J M W Turner painted his view across the Ouse in about 1830.

A long, sprawling building, the church shows work of most centuries from the 12th to the 19th. The fine proportions of the 14th-century chancel are worthy of note, as are its renewed east window

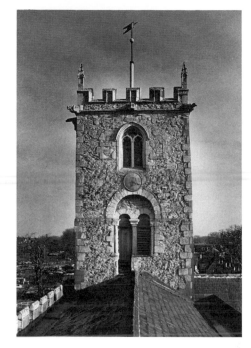

containing good 19th-century glass by Clayton & Bell and its wall monuments of the 17th to the 19th centuries. A remarkable air of antiquity is given to the church by the jumble of roof slopes on the north side out of which rises the tower.

8 Edworth, St George
TL 222 407

East of the Great North Road and just south of Biggleswade, St George's can be seen across the fields in a peaceful location, but near a busy farmyard. The tower is ancient and the original building dates from around 1200. Tower and nave are crenellated and on each side there is a handsome porch with a short east aisle. During the Middle Ages St George's association with St Neots Priory probably accounted for the unexpectedly high quality of the carving in the porches, the arcades, the font, pillar piscina, choir stalls and elsewhere. There is also good medieval glass.

9 Farndish, St Michael
SP 928 638

Although old buildings in this part of England – Farndish is four miles southeast of Wellingborough – often have almost orange local stone, here there are only occasional stones of this colour, except for the doorway, where it alternates with a more typical grey stone. These polychrome effects from about 1210 would have delighted William Butterfield.

Nave and chancel are basically 13th-century but the tracery in the windows is 14th-century and the tower was built inside the nave in the 15th. The label stops – terminating the decoration around the windows – are attractively carved. Within all is simplicity, with more carvings, mid-19th-century oak furnishings and a sense of deep peace, but not, as can so easily happen, of desolation. A place for prayer.

10 Little Barford, St Denys
TL 178 569

From the south as one approaches from Tempsford, the aisle-less nave and west tower of St Denys present an embattled look, with windows from at least three centuries. The attractive south doorway from the original Norman church remains. The arcade of the north aisle may be dated *c*.1300, when the nave was substantially rebuilt. The church must have been heightened in the 15th century, when the clerestory was made and a stage added to the west tower. There are a Perpendicular screen, a brass of 1535 and a chancel of 1869 by Blomfield with excellent original furnishings and decoration.

St Denys stands isolated amid fields and cows, almost drowned by cow parsley in early summer, with the roar of the A1 some distance to the west and, until recently, a large modern power station to the north.

11 Lower Gravenhurst, St Mary
TL 111 352

The modest exterior of this small church between Bedford and Hitchin gives little indication of the charm of its interior, which still remains virtually as it was in the 14th century. The nave and chancel the chancel screen, the pews and the king-post roof have all survived from that time. The tower with its unusual cross in place of a spire was added in the 15th century. The interior still conveys the sense of a *mysterium tremendum et fascinans*.

As with so many other churches coming to the Fund, Lower Gravenhurst owes much – perhaps its survival – to a devoted lady parishioner, in this case Miss Mercy Collisson. For nearly forty years she organised musical recitals in the church in the summer months. We hope these will continue and will be imitated elsewhere.

12 Pottesgrove, St Mary
SP 951 298

Pottesgrove church is to be found down a cul-de-sac beyond an unexpectedly bleak stretch of land south of Woburn. The churchyard contains some fine headstones.

The building dates from the early 14th century and has a three-bay nave and two-bay chancel. Of this date are the rood screen, the north and south doorways and some of the stained glass in the west window. The nave roof is 15th- or early 16th-century.

All this needs to be emphasised for, at first glance, the church appears to be Victorian. It was extensively restored in 1880 by J D Sedding, who was closely involved with the Arts and Crafts movement. To him are due the high pitched roof, the door ironwork, the font and furnishings, the arrangement of old glass in the west window and the spirelet offset to the north.

BERKSHIRE

13 East Shefford, St Thomas
SU 391 747

This small church stands in idyllic surroundings close to the River Lambourn, a little to the north of the M4, west of Newbury. It is Saxon or early Norman in origin, with a 13th-century chancel and later windows, is largely constructed of flint, and rendered. There are a brick porch and a little bell-turret at the west end.

The interior is full of interest. Above the chancel arch is one of the earliest remaining schemes of wall-painting in the country, conserved by Mrs Eve Baker in 1971–6. On the walls are texts and consecration crosses. There are fine memorials to the Fettiplace family, a Norman tub-font and some old glass.

About 1960 the Friends of Friendless Churches were instrumental in saving the church from neglect, if not demolition. Going into it today, and savouring its stillness and the long history which it wears with so much grace, it is scarcely believable that such an intervention was ever needed.

14 Lower Basildon, St Bartholomew
SU 612 793

Lying between the River Thames and the main Great Western Railway line, west of Reading, the old church of Basildon is

some distance from its village and even further from the now more populous village of Upper Basildon. The main part of the church is built of knapped flint and belongs chiefly to the early Decorated period. The chancel is taller than the nave and with its beautiful traceried windows is of superb quality both in design and construction. The Georgian brick tower is an attractive foil to the rest of the building. In 1875–6 the church was subject to a thorough restoration, the best feature of which was perhaps the elaborate south porch.

Fine monuments to the Sykes family include one each by John Flaxman and R Brown, and the remarkable early-19th-century memorial outside which makes use of a 14th-century canopy.

BUCKINGHAMSHIRE

15 Broughton, St Lawrence
SP 894 401

Broughton is a rural enclave lying just within the boundary of Milton Keynes yet retaining its original individuality.

The church consists of an early 15th century west tower, a nave and chancel displaying early-14th-century features and an 18th-century south porch. That no aisles were subsequently added has enabled an important series of wall-paintings in the nave to survive to a greater extent than in many other churches. They were uncovered in 1849 and depict the Last Judgement, the Deposition, St George, St Eligius and St Helena.

16   Edlesborough, St Mary the Virgin
TL 970 191

Edlesborough is as hard to hide as many Fund churches are to find. It stands high on a hillock beside the A4147 south-east

of Leighton Buzzard, a large building of local limestone. It has been patched over the years with flint, brick and other materials so that it now looks slightly leprous – too true an analogy, for the limestone is soft and is visibly eroding in this exposed situation.

The tower of 1340 is massive and the church is in scale with it. Large windows with prettily leaded but obscured glass, high arcades and aisles, and splendid 15th-century woodwork make it seem a mini-cathedral. Screen, pulpit, tester, misericords, stalls and choir desks and most of the roofs are all medieval and of very good quality. Sadly the best misericord and the famous rose brass have both been stolen, but enough remains – medieval and 19th-century tiles, brasses, a Kempe window and a good Victorian scheme of wall decoration – to reward those who climb the hillock.

17   Fleet Marston, St Mary
SP 779 159

Few of the motorists who dash along the A41 between Aylesbury and Waddesdon notice a little building standing on a hillock in a field near the road where Wesley preached one of his first sermons after ordination; and indeed, the circle of trees with which it is girdled conceals it even from the pedestrian.

It is a church consisting of nave and chancel built in the 12th and 13th centuries with a charming interior. The chancel arch was rebuilt in the 14th century and in the nave is a fine queen-post roof of the 15th century. The church was sensitively restored by Sir George Gilbert Scott in 1868.

18 Hartwell, The Assumption
SP 795 125

Regrettably this is only a ghost of former glory. The church was built on the site of the medieval church for Sir William Lee of Hartwell House by Henry Kenee in 1754–6. It is in the form of an octagon with towers at each end and has been called 'a classical design in fancy dress'.

Originally the interior was resplendent with fan-tracery vaulting in plaster and more good plasterwork on the walls. The theft of lead from the roof left all this at the mercy of the elements and vandals destroyed what remained. Now there is but an empty, roofless shell, with odd bits of debris giving hints of the glory which has departed.

19 Pitstone, St Mary
SP 942 150

Pitstone sits below the Chilterns in chalk country. From the first church on this site, founded about 1180, only the beautifully carved font remains. The present church dates partly from the late 13th century and consists of west tower, nave and chancel, with an aisle to both. The handsomely carved capitals in the chancel are of the 13th century but there was substantial rebuilding around 1450–70, including the austere nave arcade. There are an unusually large number of medieval tiles, some vigorous stone carving and a small brass, probably of the wife of Sir John Neyrnut in whose time the church was enlarged.

The pews are mainly early 16th-century; the fine pulpit and table were installed after a critical archdeacon's visitation in 1637. The Royal Arms, Lord's Prayer and Ten Commandments above the chancel arch are dated 1733. 19th-century restoration tended to leave well alone so there remains still a strong medieval feel about St Mary's.

CAMBRIDGESHIRE

20 Abbotsley, St Margaret
TL 227 565

This large church is to be found four miles south-east of St Neots. The chancel is still the parish church, the remainder of the building being in the care of the Fund. The Tilly family are said to have paid for the construction of the church in the 13th or early 14th century. There is an elaborate tomb in a recess in the south aisle which probably commemorates one of them.

The tower is slightly later and is the church's main glory, with statues at the corners. They are said to be of William the Conqueror, Harold, Macbeth and Malcolm, whose wife Margaret was canonised in 1250. The Scots connection is less far-fetched than it may seem since the Kings of Scotland were Earls of Huntingdon in the peerage of England.

The 19th-century restoration – a sensitive one – was by William Butterfield, who also designed many of the furnishings.

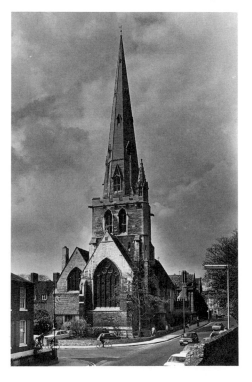

21 Cambridge, All Saints

Above the chancel of All Saints soar the tower and spire, landmarks in this part of Cambridge. This fine church, opposite the great gate of Jesus College, was built in 1863–70 to replace the medieval church of All Saints-in-the-Jewry. Its architect was G F Bodley (d. 1907) one of the most gifted and sensitive of all 19th-century church architects. Constructed of hand-made brick, faced with Northamptonshire oolitic limestone, it consists of a nave, south aisle, north porch and chancel, with south organ chamber and vestry.

The interior is remarkable for its unity of design, colour and ornament. The fine glass in the east window is by William Morris & Co., some of the twenty figures being by Morris, others by Burne-Jones and Ford Maddox Brown. The stencilled decoration of the walls and painted ceiling are now considered to have been designed in two stages. First, in 1870 C R

Kempe designed the ceiling decoration, executed by F R Leach. Then, in 1878 the wall stencils were designed by Bodley and executed by Leach. Bodley also designed most of the other fittings: the alabaster font, the pulpit, the oak screens of the aisle and chancel.

22 Cambridge, St Peter
TF 445 591

Lying at the north end of Cambridge, St Peter's was demolished in 1781 and rebuilt on the western part of the former nave. The 14th-century tower and spire at the west end survive from the earlier church. At the time of rebuilding, a 12th-century doorway was reset in the north wall and an early 13th-century doorway in the south wall. Inside is a remarkable carved 11th-century font.

St Peter's adjoins Kettle's Yard which was established by Mr H S Ede as a museum, art gallery and unique concert centre for the University; it still flourishes and is widely known. The church owes much to Mr Ede's daily watch and generous care and his successors have maintained this tradition. There is a real atmosphere of prayer about the church and the visitors' book shows that St Peter's is a place of pilgrimage for people of all faiths. One hopes that more of the Fund's churches will be rediscovered and come to have the same unique and moving atmosphere as this one.

23 Conington, All Saints
TL 181 859

The fine pinnacles of Conington can be seen from the Great North Road (ten miles north of Huntingdon) or from the Kings Cross to Edinburgh railway line; closer inspection does not disappoint. This is one of the few medieval churches built all-in-one at the end of the 15th century with only minor embellishments later.

The nave, chancel and the noble west tower are all of this date, though the pinnacles are of 1638. The style is austere and handsome rather than gracious. The large late-Gothic windows give plenty of light and the fine pews and other furnishings – mostly provided by the Heathcotes in 1841, (the Reverend George Heathcote being rector 1834–84) reinforce the impact of the architecture through their uniformity. The north and south doors retain their original ironwork.

Conington is famous for its monuments; those to King David and Prince Henry of Scotland remind us that the kings of Scotland were Earls of Huntingdon in the peerage of England. There are three centuries of Cottons, including the famous 17th-century antiquary Sir Robert, whose collection is in the British Museum. Grinling Gibbons is thought to have carved the bust of Elizabeth Cotton in the north aisle and the monument to her husband, Sir John, in the north chapel. There is another Cotton memorial at Steeple Gidding, close at hand.

The early 13th-century effigy of a Franciscan, with helmet of mail, in the south chapel, may be that of Bernard de Brus – a link with the Fund's church at Skelton in Cleveland.

24 Duxford, St John
TL 478 462

The 13th-century tower of St John's, can be seen from afar, just east of the M11, and capped by a 'candle snuffer' lead spire. The church has been largely unused since 1874 and has at times been nearly ruinous.

The Norman nave has three internal arches with beautifully carved and moulded capitals and bases. The chancel is 13th-century. The Lady Chapel, which opens to the north, contains high quality 14th-century work, particularly the 'flamboyant' tracery of the east window, the carved stone corbels and the niches. When the nave was rebuilt in the 15th century the north aisle and the wooden south porch were added.

Above the inner south doorway is a 7th- or 8th-century tympanum of Celtic or Northumbrian work. There are medieval pews in the tower and crossing, the chancel has a 15th-century carved roof and the altar-table and communion-rails are Stuart. Remarkable too is the amount of medieval graffiti. There is a series of 12th- and 13th-century wall-paintings which may well, when fully revealed, be comparable with neighbouring Ickleton.

25 Guyhirn Chapel
TF 403 040

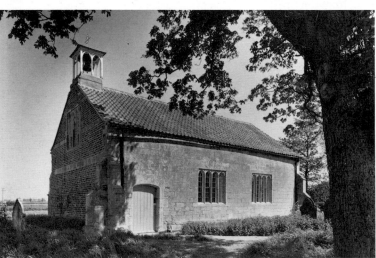

Five miles south-west of Wisbech, the chapel is close to the A47. Built in 1660, this little chapel was overtaken by the restoration of the monarchy; but neither the returning Stuarts nor the restoring Victorians altered its austere puritan appearance. It remains essentially simple, with brick and stone walls and floor. The narrow pews remain unsuitable for Popish kneeling but dedicated to hearing the Word – and the inattentive could see through the clear glass windows the wonder, terror and infinity of the bleak Fenland world outside.

For a time, Guyhirn was a centre for Huguenot exiles from France. The chapel is lovingly cared for by its neighbours and its rescue was enthusiastically supported by John Betjeman.

26 Long Stanton, St Michael
TF 403 658

Just north-west of Cambridge, this small thatched church is set in one of the barer stretches of the county. It is a Grade-A listed building, with the chancel dating from the early 13th century and the nave from the mid-13th century. About 1300 the aisles and walls were rebuilt and the roof of the nave and aisles appears to have been made continuous at that time.

The chancel was rebuilt in 1884 but older material was reused and an unusual 13th-century double piscina was incorporated into it. Like a cadet branch of an old family, St Michael's has had more imitators than many of the more famous churches in the Fund's care – particularly in the United States near Philadelphia and in South Dakota.

Drawing by Robert Speechley, who was responsible for the repairs in 1884.

27 Offord D'Arcy, St Peter
TL 217 664

The two Offord villages – Cluny and D'Arcy – adjoin each other near the Great Ouse between Huntington and St Neots and each has a medieval church. Between the churches and the river, and very close indeed to this church, runs the Kings Cross to Edinburgh main line.

The church has a fabric of typically mixed medieval materials of varying dates. The north arcade is Norman, the chancel early English, the south aisle 14th-century and the clerestory 15th-century. The walls are of local cobble-rubble.

Inside are the beautifully carved remains of a screen, which was formerly part of a parclose but is now fixed to the chancel arch. There are also a fine piscina and a Victorian-Jacobean chancel roof. The chief monument is to Richard Nailour, his two wives, two sons and six daughters and was carved in 1616.

28 Parson Drove, St John the Baptist
TF 390 091

This fine Fenland church, four miles west of Wisbech, has much surviving from

medieval times and deserves to see more of the visitors who go to more celebrated churches nearby. The nave of seven bays and the west tower with its fine arch and vaulted ceiling are 15th-century. The north aisle has a 13th-century doorway and 14th-century windows. The south aisle was largely rebuilt around 1800, while tradition has it that the chancel was destroyed by a flood in 1613.

Inside there is an octagonal font of the Perpendicular period. The pulpit is dated 1677. The windows are large and of clear glass with medieval heraldic glass in the tracery. Everywhere there are delightful carvings to be discovered – turn round and you will find a medieval face looking at you. Look too at the remarkable collection of carved gravestones in the churchyard.

29 Steeple Gidding, St Andrew
TL 132 813

St Andrew's is a lesser known neighbour to the nearby famous and tranquil Little Gidding church. It is a simple and nearly empty building with a feeling of the Middle Ages which was prolonged by the sympathetic restoration of Arthur Blomfield in 1874. Basically it is a 14th-century building with a south doorway made of 12th- and 14th-century stone. The spire with its lucarnes is like a small scale edition of the great Northamptonshire spires. Inside is a Cotton memorial which links the church to that at Conington, across the Great North Road.

30   Swaffham Prior, St Cyriac and St Julitta
TF 568 639

A fine tall 14th-century octagonal tower, based on the central tower of Ely Cathedral, distinguishes this Grade-1 church, which is six miles east of Cambridge. The nave and chancel were rebuilt in local brick in 1806, providing an elegant and spacious interior, which contrasts with the strange, haunting quality of the tower.

The church shares a churchyard with the equally large St Mary's, reflecting no doubt the jurisdiction of different manors in the Middle Ages. The two towers vie with each other but it is St Cyriac's which can claim pre-eminence. The parish still uses its fine 1791 ring of bells to summon the faithful.

CHESHIRE

31 Macclesfield, Christ Church
SJ 914 736

A large town church, built in 1775–6, it contains almost all its original box-pews in the nave, aisles and gallery; and all too

little original clear glass in its windows. It was built at the expense of Charles Roe, who played a prominent part in the development of the Macclesfield silk industry in the 18th century and whose monument, by John Bacon, is in the chancel. The church is built of brick, with cast-iron columns supporting the gallery and was said by some to be capable of conversion to a silk mill.

Roe appointed as first vicar David Simpson, a friend of John Wesley. Christ Church played a significant part in the Evangelical Revival, and Simpson's appointment was a challenge to the conventional church of the day, matching the physical challenge to the old parish church posed by Christ Church's very tall tower.

CLEVELAND

32 Skelton in Cleveland, All Saints Old Church
NZ 653 191

Hauntingly illustrated in Mark Chatfield's *Churches the Victorians Forgot* (1979), All Saints stands in the park at the west end of Skelton (ten miles east of Middlesbrough), on a site where there were probably two previous churches. A new church was built more centrally in 1884.

The church is substantially of 1785 with some medieval masonry and a largely medieval plan. Pulpit, box-pews (of pine grained to resemble oak) and other furnishings all appear to date from the 1785 rebuilding, with slightly earlier textboards and a number of older monuments grouped on the remaining medieval wall.

All is eminently sensible, with a strong flavour of its locality enhanced by the herringbone tooling of the external stonework.

CUMBRIA

33 Brougham, St Ninian
NY 559 299

Known locally as 'Ninekirks', this church stands in a stone-walled churchyard on the bank of the River Eamont and is approached along a many-gated track leading off the A66 between Penrith and Appleby. There are now no houses within sight of the church save one farm.

Tradition has it that St Ninian founded a church on this site in the 5th century and that villagers took refuge there when pursued by the Danes. In 1846, when the Bird burial chamber was being cleared out by Lord Brougham, a number of skeletons were discovered; with one of these was buried a silver gilt cup mount, on which the ornamentation may well be of Pictish manufacture. The burial dates from the Viking period.

The present church was built in 1660 by Lady Anne Clifford of Brougham Castle on the site of an earlier building which was, according to her, in parlous condition. The external appearance is very similar to the chapel which she rebuilt the previous year, close to the Castle.

St Ninian's has a long and low profile. It is of simple design with rubble walls and slate roofs, with symmetrically arranged small windows. Apart from the south porch and bell-cote which were added in 1841, the entire church and its furnishings and fittings date from the 17th century. The box pews (some magnificently canopied), pulpit, screen and communion-rails were all carefully restored about 1900. Inside, the walls are white-washed, the roof has curved braces and the floor is paved with stone flags.

34 Ireby Old Chancel
NY 224 393

Reached across a field at the bottom of a lane that in springtime is bedecked with daffodils, this is a pretty and peaceful spot, a worthy neighbour of Solway and the Cumbrian hills. The chancel is all that remains of the old church except for the font, piscina and some carved stones which were moved to the new church in 1846. The nave was then pulled down but two columns from the arcade have been reinstated to show where it stood.

The old church was built in the middle of the 12th century and the chancel extended eastwards about 1170 when the lancet windows were inserted. During a restoration in 1880 a number of the grave slabs were inserted into the walls.

DERBYSHIRE

35 Kedleston, All Saints
SK 313 404

This is a late-13th-century building with a Norman south doorway and a tower over the central crossing. The east end was made classical in appearance in the late 17th century. Most of the furnishings date from this time or slightly later – font, box-pews, communion-rails, family pews. They would stand out in a church less rich in treasures than this.

The major feature is, however, the series of monuments to the Curzon family which range from the 13th to the 20th century. Under wooden lids in the chancel floor are visible the busts of an early-14th-century mail-clad man and his wife, part of a memorial slab, probably representing Sir Richard de Curzon and his wife Joan. He is known to have held Kedleston in 1297. There are two alabaster monuments from the famous workshop at Chellaston, not far away. Other monuments were designed by Adam, Rysbrack and Scheemakers.

In 1906 G F Bodley was commissioned to design a new chapel, on the north side of the church, as a memorial to the first Lady Curzon. Here are the effigies, designed by Sir Bertram Mackennal, of Lord Curzon (d. 1925) Viceroy of India (first Marquess Curzon of Kedleston) and his first wife Mary Leiter. The chapel furnishings present an eclectic *tour de force* of holy objects.

Kedleston also has a superb collection of glass of *c*.1910, by T F Curtis of Ward and Hughes, J Powell and particularly F C Eden.

DEVON

36 Luffincott, St James
SX 335 948

Luffincott is about seven miles north of Launceston, set above the remote and beautiful wooded valley of the Tamar. The church is tucked away at the end of a long lane and across a farmyard. Of medieval origin, the nave and chancel are continuous, with an attractive barrel vault. The west tower was rebuilt in 1791 and the delightful domestic sash windows on the north side are of that date. There is a 14th-century granite font. The churchyard, which has also been vested in the Fund, possesses a fine group of five slate headstones.

37 Parracombe, St Petrock
SS 675 449

Some ten miles north-east of Barnstaple, the setting on a hill above the village in glorious countryside makes this a remarkable building. The interior is even more magical, normally bathed in light with furnishings hardly altered in 200 years.

Though the dedication indicates a pre-Saxon foundation, the oldest part of the present building is Norman. The base of the tower was built in 1182, the chancel rebuilt in 1252 and the nave reconstructed with the addition of an aisle about 1500, with roofs of the local barrel type.

The great charm of the church however is the unspoilt 18th-century interior – rails round three sides of the holy table, three-decker pulpit complete with reading desk, box-pews and musicians' seats raised on steps at the west end. The simple early chancel screen is surmounted by a solid timber tympanum decorated with the Royal Arms, the Lord's Prayer, the Ten Commandments, the Creed and the names of the church-wardens, whom the accounts show to have paid £1.11.6 'for cleansing the commandments' in 1758.

In 1879 doubts were expressed about the safety of the structure and experts

advised that it should be pulled down, but John Ruskin led a national movement in favour of building a new church and repairing the old to avoid such 'vandalism'. St Petrock's many visitors confirm how right Ruskin was.

38   Revelstoke, St Peter the Poor Fisherman
SX 564 465

The appearance of this rugged medieval church – of Saxon origin and originally cruciform – matches the charm of its dedication. The aisle and the porch have finely carved wagon roofs of the late Middle Ages, but much of the rest of the church is now roofless. The dramatic setting overlooking Stoke Bay and the church's monastic appearance make it a rare thing in England, a cross between the sort of Pyrenean cloister a Rockefeller might have transported to New York and the grittiness of a Celtic shrine.

39   Torbryan, Holy Trinity
SS 820 669

Nothing about the approach to the church through a typical south Devon landscape leads one to expect a building of such

grandeur. The tower, which was built in 1445, belongs to the famous group of towers centred on Ashburton and Totnes, both four miles away. Their distinctive feature is that for the first time the stair turret is moved to the central position on the main face and becomes the chief formal architectural element of the design. Probably as one continuous building campaign, the rest of the church was rebuilt on the same dignified scale as the tower. Finally the two-storied south porch, with its beautiful fan vault, was added.

The quality of the external design, notable in the delicacy of the medieval window tracery, is reflected in the furnishings of the late 15th century; in the screen, with painted figures of saints, spanning the church from aisle to aisle; in the medieval benches now encased by 18th-century box-pews; and in the stained glass. The altar has been made with woodwork taken from the old pulpit, and the pulpit in turn made of wood taken from the pier casings of the roodscreen. The bells are medieval.

40   West Ogwell Church

SX 819 700

Approached by winding, undulating lanes, West Ogwell has an atmosphere of remote obscurity which belies its closeness to Newton Abbot, three miles to the north-east. The church stands on a knoll, with open views across the landscape, beside the former manor house built in 1790.

It seems that the chancel and nave – which are of similar length – and the two matching transepts were built c.1300. A two-storey west tower was added to this cruciform building about 1400 and probably the south porch and the priest's door date from this time also. During the 15th century, large three-light Perpendicular windows were inserted in the east and south walls of the south transept, suggesting that this transept was used as a chantry chapel.

The church was restored in the early 19th century when a vestry was added on the north side of the nave. Inside there is a fine medieval roof. The box-pews in the nave were installed in 1823, as were the tiers of benches in front of the tower screen. There is a fine 17th-century oak pulpit and the communion-rails have an elegant curved central section.

DORSET

41 Bothenhampton, Holy Trinity Old Church
ST 475 918

At the end of a no-through road, with the Downs beyond, there is considerable magic in the situation of Holy Trinity, standing high above Bridport. Only the 13th-century chancel and 15th-century tower now survive from the medieval parish church. When the nave was demolished in 1889 and a new church – a rarity by E S Prior – built in the centre of the village, the chancel continued in use as a mortuary chapel. During recent repairs, a 17th-century inscription was revealed on the east wall, showing that the east window had been blocked up before the erection of the impressive reredos which forms a single unit with the communion-rails.

42 Nether Cerne, All Saints
SY 669 983

Nether Cerne church stands beside the manor house. It is a picturesque building of the 13th century, in a charming pastoral setting in the Cerne Valley. Tower and porch were added when the church was refashioned in the 15th century. Flint and stone, as so often in Dorset and Wiltshire, blend delightfully in the tower which is crowned by vigorous carving. The font has a 12th-century bowl which presumably survives from an earlier church on the site.

43 Oborne, St Cuthbert Old Church
ST 653 178

All that survives of Oborne's old church is the chancel, built in 1553 according to an inscription over the east window, sandwiched now between the main A30 road and the Waterloo to Exeter railway line. It must have been one of the last pre-Reformation churches to be built and marked the elevation of Oborne to parochial status. Its first incumbent was sacristan to Sherborne Abbey and he is commemorated in an inscription over the north window. There are medieval sliptiles, a pillar piscina, which is not original to the church; and communion-rails, pulpit and monuments, both in the church and the churchyard, all of the 17th century.

44 Portland, St George Reforne
SY 686 720

This cruciform church was built in 1758 by Thomas Gilbert. The tower bears a striking resemblance to the west towers of St Paul's cathedral and it is probably significant that Gilbert's grandfather had been surveyor to the quarries when Wren was building St Paul's.

The twin pulpits and lecterns survive intact as do the box-pews and galleries. It is a singularly complete interior of its date. In the large churchyard are about 400 tombstones, many of naval interest, with fascinating inscriptions. The church is in a bleak situation on the top of the island, a parable of man's thirsty rationality literally pitted against the winds and other furies of nature.

This was one of the churches chosen by the Bridges Commission in 1960 to illustrate the type of church which might come to the Fund.

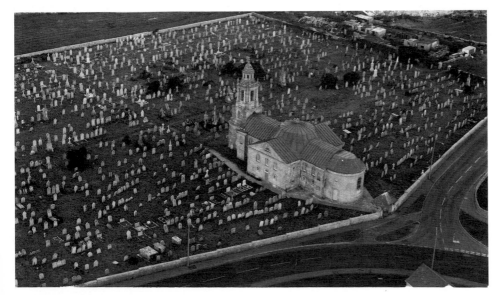

45 Stockwood, St Edwold
ST 590 069

South of Yeovil, just to the east of the A37, down a farm road with the farmhouse on the right and an old footbridge in front, is St Edwold's, surrounded by hills and woods. This church measures only 30ft by 12ft 8in and is one of the smallest in England. Built early in the 15th century, it was probably not the first church on this site – the unique dedication to an Anglian saint suggests a pre-Norman foundation.

The west porch and delightful bell-turret were added in 1636. Unfortunately, a Victorian restoration caused the piscina to be reset outside the chancel and removed the old furnishings.

46 Tarrant Crawford, St Mary the Virgin
ST 924 035

Beyond the slight remains of Tarrant Abbey, a celebrated Cistercian nunnery, the church of St Mary the Virgin stands solitary on the hillside at the end of a lane. The varied materials in the walls give the church a very particular texture.

The chancel is 12th-century, the nave 13th- and on the south wall is an important series of paintings from the 14th. There is a thin, slightly later, west tower. Many of the furnishings date from the 17th and 18th centuries, all comprising an interior of great charm and antiquarian interest in a remarkable setting. It has a powerful feel of Thomas Hardy, with its rustic simplicity (the wall-paintings were uncovered after the novels were written) and a strong hint of the ghost of the Abbey.

But best of all, perhaps, is the setting, in a field beside the A352 just outside Dorchester.

47 Whitcombe
SY 716 883

William Barnes, author of three volumes of poems in the Dorset dialect, was appointed vicar here after his his ordination in 1847 and, a few years later, was appointed to Winterborne Came, another Fund church, only a mile away.

This church stands on a pre-Conquest site and contains two fragments of Saxon crosses. The nave is 12th-century, partly rebuilt in the 18th, and the font 13th. The chancel was built in the 15th, reusing the old east window, and the tower appears, from an inscription on one of the louvres, to have been completed in or by 1596.

The church is also famous for its wall-paintings – early consecration crosses, an arcade of niches dating from about 1300 and a superb St Christopher, which is probably about 100 years later.

48 Winterborne Came, St Peter
SY 705 884

Just outside Dorchester and close to the Fund's church at Whitcombe, St Peter's is also associated with William Barnes (1801–86), who lived in the thatched rectory here and is remembered for his collections of poems in the Dorset dialect. He is buried in the churchyard. All around are echoes of Thomas Hardy, a friend of Barnes.

The situation close to the Palladian Came House and alongside some of its associated outbuildings is almost the epitome of the country squire's church. It is a simple building – a 14th-century nave with chancel added early in the 15th. The chancel screen is 16th-century but much restored. A large 1611 tomb-chest to John Mellor with two recumbent figures, together with other memorials and furnishings, give evidence of affection and care through many centuries.

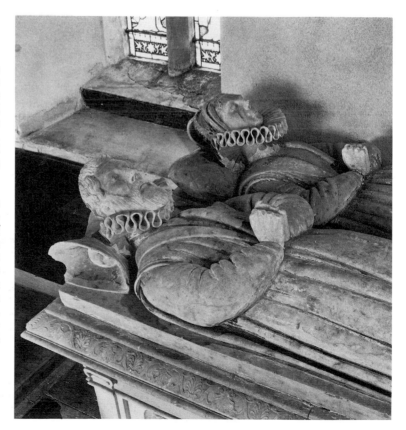

49 Winterborne Tomson, St Andrew
SY 885 974

This delightful apsidal church is 11th-century in origin, and now dominated within by the box-pews and other furnishings presented in the early 18th century by William Wake, Archbishop of Canterbury (d. 1737). The gallery is probably 16th-century and may have been the rood loft before it was removed. Over the years the oak has bleached to a magical silvery grey. The south wall has three 17th-century windows and one much earlier one; the north wall is blind.

It was gently repaired in 1932 by A R Powys, Secretary for the Society for the Protection of Ancient Buildings, using the proceeds from the sale of Thomas Hardy's manuscripts. Hardy was an architect's assistant in this area and the church remains as in the days of which he wrote. With its early apse, its vernacular barrel roof, its rational and Protestant pews, it reflects most vividly the passing centuries. Its calm says something to ours.

ESSEX

There is now a wall between the church and Audley Chapel

50 Berechurch, St Michael, Audley Chapel
TL 993 219

The Audley Chapel is a 16th-century brick addition on the north side of the former St Michael's church, Berechurch, which lies in an isolated and wooded position two miles south of Colchester. The church itself is in private ownership.

The chapel is notable for its superb contemporary hammerbeam roof with richly carved timbers and later decoration with the arms of the Audley and Walden families. There is a fine series of 17th-century monuments to members of the Audley family and a notable wrought-iron railing of the same period divides the chapel from the church.

51 Chickney, St Mary
TL 575 280

Most of the walls of this isolated church are pre-Conquest and double-splayed windows of that period may be seen on each side of the nave. In the 13th century the chancel was extended eastwards and in the 14th the tower was added, together with more windows on each side of the nave – it must have been a very dark building before that. Of this date also are the nave roof and the doorway.

The richly carved font and the squint to the north of the chancel arch are both 15th-century. The altar stone or mensa is 13th-century as is the piscina.

This is a gentle building of great antiquity, which has escaped the fiercer forms of restoration and is the better for it. The churchyard adjoins the neighbouring manor house and gives a feeling of English peace and remoteness.

52 Colchester, St Leonard at the Hythe
TM 013 247

St Leonard's was the church of the old port of Colchester, and is now in an area with few residents. Nave, chancel and north aisle date from 1330–40 with a 15th-century south arcade, aisle and porch. The tower is late-14th-century; a rather high-spirited late-Victorian top survived an earthquake in 1884 only to be damaged in the great storm of 1987.

The hammerbeam nave roof is 16th-century and over the chancel arch is a 19th-century Annunciation, part of a decorative scheme which 1943 photographs show to have been all over the church. Stained glass and fittings are generally of the same period, making a lovingly cared for, handsome Tractarian interior.

53　East Horndon, All Saints
TQ 636 894

For some five centuries this hilltop church, a landmark above the Southend road, was associated with the Tyrell family and its most valued possession is the limestone memorial slab to Lady Alice Tyrell (d. 1422). Her husband, Sir John Tyrell, was Speaker of the House of Commons and fought at Agincourt. Her son built this church, unusually in brick, during the Wars of the Roses. Only the north wall of the chancel survives from the older building and is probably Norman. The porch and the door date from about 1500. The low west tower was originally built in c.1475 but has since been rebuilt.

After frequent thefts and acts of vandalism in the 1960s, vigorous action by local well-wishers and the parish of Layer Marney in 1970 led to the rescue of the building and its eventual vesting in the Fund. Evening Communion services and excellent concerts are now held.

54　Halstead, Holy Trinity
TL 808 305

This is an early (1844) work by Gilbert Scott. Outside it is very severe, Early English, done in flint with pale East Anglian brick quoins. The tower and spire are at the south side, standing above the porch. They form a handsome feature of the landscape on the edge of this north Essex market town.

Those who are drawn to the church by its spire and not put off by the severity of its exterior, will find an interior full of grace, warm coloured brick and stone contrasting with limewash. Emphatic capitals on the alternately round and octagonal columns in the arcades punctuate the vertical lines of the high nave.

All reveals the hand of a substantial architect.

55 West Bergholt, St Mary Old Church
TL 954 281

Surely, one is tempted to write, this is a 14th-century church, but then one stops and looks harder. A Saxon door is to be seen in the north wall and much of the wall itself is of this date; some of the timbers in the bell-tower (evidently reused) are Anglo-Saxon. The charming tower itself is 15th-century, and many of its windows were remade in the 18th when the village was already beginning to move elsewhere.

The mixture of centuries is equally apparent inside the building, with a fine 18th-century west gallery and a Jacobean Royal Arms over the chancel arch. Flint walls with some brick, the timber tower, big tiled roofs and a certain eccentricity in its fenestration all combine to make St Mary's a typical, jumbly, English parish church. With the neighbouring Hall it makes a delightful ensemble.

GLOUCESTERSHIRE

56 Didmarton, St Lawrence
ST 823 874

Didmarton is a small village on the A433 road between Tetbury and Chipping Sodbury. The church stands next to the Manor in an attractive churchyard containing some 18th-century tomb-chests and several mature trees.

Consisting of nave and chancel under one roof, north transept and south porch, the church is of medieval origin refashioned in the 18th century. The transept is surmounted by a charming wooden bell-turret.

The interior of the church is an uncommon and important example of Georgian liturgical arrangement, fortuitously preserved by the fact that the Victorians built a new church nearby. The 18th-century work includes a three-decker pulpit and elegant reredos, all in pale apple green contrasting with the white walls. Box-pews remain to north and south of the sanctuary and may have been assigned to children and communicants.

57 Eastleach Martin, St Michael and St Martin
SP 202 052

Through deep country lanes, two miles off the main road between Burford and Lechlade, lies the double village of East-leach Martin and Eastleach Turville. On each side of the River Leach, only about 200 yards apart, stand two churches. St Michael's is set in a sloping churchyard on the east of the river, flanked to the south by an ancient barn and with a wooded hill looming above the lane on the eastern boundary. A footpath crosses the river by Keble's Bridge, a reminder of the long links of this family with the village to which John Keble came as a curate after ordination in 1815.

Though early Norman in origin, much of the building is 13th-century, and under-went some restoration in the 1880s. The low-pitched pyramidal roof of the tower with its weathercock is a distinctive feature.

Built of local stone rubble and roofed with local stone slates, the church con-sists of nave and chancel, with a west tower only just surmounting the ridge of the nave, and a north transept containing three most beautiful late-13th-century windows, that on the north having five lights with cusped intersecting tracery. All the windows of the transept have hood moulds with carved stops.

Inside are a Perpendicular octagonal font, a hexagonal pulpit made up of 17th- and 18th-century panelling, a lectern made from Elizabethan domestic furniture and square-ended oak pews of the 16th and 17th centuries.

58 Gloucester, St Nicholas
SO 829 188

From the city itself and from the bypass, the truncated spire of the church is a familiar landmark. It was built about 1450 but subsidence made it necessary to dismantle the top of the spire in 1783, replacing it with the present coronet; further substantial repair took place in 1987.

The church is originally 11th- or 12th-century, the oldest visible parts being the western end of the north arcade and the south doorway. Most of the building is 13th-century, with larger windows added later. The tower with fine lierne vault and the east and south aisle windows are 15th-century.

There are many monuments and memo-rial slabs commemorating significant citizens of Gloucester. (The Mayor would use St Nicholas rather than the Cathedral when relations with the Dean and Chap-ter were strained.) The most important is the tomb of Alderman John Walton and his wife Alice (1626), a splendid example of municipal self-confidence.

Also there is a Jacobean former gallery-front and an unusual arrangement of squints to enable people in the aisles to see the sanctuary. The Royal Arms are those of Charles II. The 14th-century bronze closing ring from the south door is now in the City Museum.

The spire before 1783.

59 Lassington, St Oswald Tower
SO 796 212

Only the tower of St Oswald's survives. Though probably of Saxon origin, the church is known to have been rebuilt in 1095 and the two lower stages of the tower are certainly early Norman. The body of the church, which was rebuilt in 1874–75 in the Norman style, has been demolished.

60 Little Washbourne, St Mary
SO 990 340

Set in an orchard, this delightful vernacular church has a small central turret and massive sloping buttresses on each side. It is six miles east of Tewkesbury. The walls are of warm local stone, with slate roofs to match. Inside are a Norman chancel arch and broadly splayed window, some traces of medieval wall-painting, just one tablet in the chancel and a complete, elegant set of 18th-century furnishings – holy table, pulpit and pews, lit through 18th-century windows.

All said in a few words. Perfection needs no more.

61 Ozleworth, St Nicholas of Myra
ST 794 933

Reached along the drive to Ozleworth House, the church is in a remote and beautiful setting in the south Cotswolds, east of Wotton-under-Edge and near the Cotswold Way. The surrounding circular churchyard suggests an early, if not pre-Christian, site and contains several good 18th- and 19th-century examples of typical Gloucestershire monuments.

Consisting of a nave with south porch, central tower and chancel, the church has walls and roofs of local limestone. The irregular hexagonal tower of 1110–20 is thought to be the only one surviving in this position in the country and is considered to have been the nave of the original church. About 1220 a small nave was added to the west of the tower and the chancel, presumably replacing an apse, was extended to its present length.

In 1873 a restoration was carried out by the Reverend W H Lowder and most of the nave and chancel windows were renewed and the nave lengthened.

Inside, the 12th-century crossing arch from the nave to the tower is a great rarity with deeply undercut and pierced chevrons. By contrast the Norman chancel arch is simple. French influence is apparent in the extraordinary Transitional south doorway which has very finely carved stiff-leaf foliage. The internal aspect of nave and chancel is largely the result of Lowder's restoration. There are a 13th-century font, and wall monuments of the late 18th and 19th centuries.

62 Shorncote, All Saints
SU 025 967

All Saints is a small Cotswold church just south of Cirencester and not far from the source of the Thames. Its date is about 1170, with some alterations in the 13th century and an unusual, rather later, central bell-cote. It was sensitively restored by Butterfield in 1883.

There are many little details to note – the niche in the chancel, the masonry pattern wall-paintings, 15th-century doors in the chancel arch, stone Royal Arms, a little old glass. This is a rewarding if undemonstrative building.

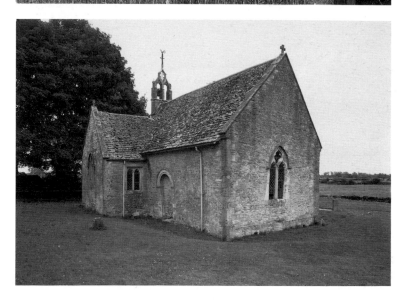

63 Tetbury, St Saviour
ST 888 933

St Saviour's was built in 1848 to serve those who could not afford pew rents at the parish church. It is constructed of local stone with Cotswold slates on the roof (to have used any other material in Tetbury would have been criminal), and its furnishings could be called 'Ecclesiological Society Enthusiastic'.

The architect was Samuel Whitfield Daukes who was assisted by Augustus Welby Pugin and John Hardman. The result is delightful – real architecture and craftsmanship.

HAMPSHIRE

64 Ashley, St Mary
SU 385 309

The hamlet of Ashley lies six miles west of Winchester near the Roman road to Old Sarum. The church has a dramatic set-

ting, lying within the outer earthworks of Gains Castle, the motte of which adjoins the churchyard to the south. The large trees round the motte rise above the church and the well-preserved inner ditch forms a boundary to the churchyard.

Mainly of Norman date, the church is of local stone, flint and brick, and covered with old lime rendering. It is a long and exceptionally narrow building consisting only of nave and chancel, the bells being hung within arches in the west gable. Inside, the impression of length is enhanced by the triple chancel arch. On either side of the Norman arch a later arch has been opened but without reaching ground level. Other features of interest include a 13th-century wall-painting in the splay of the window in the south wall of the chancel, the ancient south door and a curious tall alms box in the shape of a hollowed-out pillar.

65 Colemore, St Peter ad Vincula
SU 706 308

The church is situated in Gilbert White and Jane Austen country, six miles south of Alton. Built originally in the 12th century, from which date the aisleless nave and north transept survive, this upland church has had a stormy history. In 1308 the Bishop declared that, unless it received immediate attention, it would be beyond repair, and 300 years later it was described as being in ruins. In the 19th century extensive repairs were carried out and the chancel was rebuilt. Nevertheless in 1968 it was reported that the bell-turret was breaking up and that the building was in a bad state of repair. But it was too good to lose and the fittings, which include a Norman Purbeck marble font and a 16th-century screen, are notable.

66 Eldon, St John the Baptist
SU 365 278

It is tempting to think that this remote and tiny church west of Winchester has survived from the 12th century by being so inconspicuous. Like half a dozen churches in our care, it stands close to a farmyard but very little else. There was a substantial restoration and reduction in size in 1729 when it was very dilapidated. This happened again in the 1860s and again a hundred years later; but it now looks as well cared for as its surroundings. Traces can be found of nine consecration crosses from its original construction.

67 Freefolk, St Nicholas
SU 494 483

Basically 13th-century, this charming small church just east of Whitchurch occupies the site of a church mentioned in the Domesday Book and the origins may be much earlier. The present windows are 15th-century and so is the chancel screen, which is now at the west end forming the front of the family pew.

At the beginning of the 18th century the interior was remodelled. The central part of the reredos then introduced is now fixed to the south wall. The communion-rails and Royal Arms date from that period.

The main feature of the building is the 1614 monument to Sir Richard Powlett. On the north wall there are three super-imposed layers of wall-paintings.

68 Hartley Wintney, St Mary
SU 768 558

This village, ten miles east of Basingstoke and well known to motorists on the A30, has a charming medieval church set on a hill with splendid views. The nave and the chancel were built in the 13th century, the north and south transepts added early in the 19th century and the present flint tower built in 1842. Galleries and box-pews of the early 19th century fill the interior. The chancel fittings are earlier and on the wall are texts associated with the 1843 alterations. There are good hatchments and a Royal Arms of 1705.

In the churchyard are the graves of the architect W R Lethaby and of Field Marshal Lord Alanbrooke.

69 Itchen Stoke, St Mary
SU 559 323

This amazing church, a few miles east of Winchester, was built by Henry Conybeare in 1866 and is one of the Fund's most lively examples of Victorian architecture. It took the place of a 12th-century church a few hundred yards to the south on the old Pilgrims Way from Winchester to Canterbury. It is apsidal, very lofty, and clearly influenced by the Sainte Chapelle in Paris. The cast-iron tracery in the pulpit, the stained glass and the panels of the pews make an outstandingly complete composition. The 13th-century font survives from the earlier church.

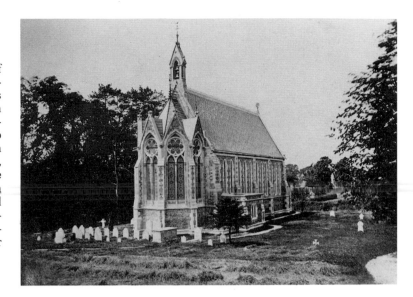

70 Little Somborne, All Saints
SU 383 326

In a downland valley south of Stockbridge, the church is little but full of charm with its wooden bell-cote, a large house beyond and a few others in the surroundings.

Mentioned in Domesday, evidence of the church's Saxon origins can be seen in the double-splayed windows in the nave – blocked in the 12th century when the chancel was extended. The plaster reveals are a thousand years old. There was a 13th-century hermit's cell at the north-east end, possibly that of Peter de Rivalles, a benefactor of Mottisfont Abbey.

The bell is Elizabethan and the splay of the 13th-century south-east window was lowered to form a fire-place in the 18th century.

71 Preston Candover, St Mary the Virgin Old Church
SU 603 414

All that remains is the chancel, the rest having been demolished when Arthur Blomfield's new church was built in 1884–5. A lancet window indicates the date of its foundation (c.1190) but few of the medieval elements survived a fire in 1681. From the 18th century there are traces of wall-paintings. There are some medieval tiles and, for so small a space, a large number of 18th-century memorial stones.

The church as it was before 1883.

72 Privett, Holy Trinity
SU 677 270

Privett church spire is a prominent and unusual landmark in the Hampshire countryside. On reaching it the visitor may be surprised to find a large late-19th-century suburban-style church standing in a deeply rural area not much altered since Gilbert White wrote about it. This magnificent edifice, designed by Sir Arthur Blomfield and built at the expense of Sir William Nicholson, the distiller, in 1876–8, replaced the small rustic church which stood nearby.

The sumptuously appointed chancel with its mosaic floor conveys the quality of the whole. Although the nave and aisles no longer have all their furnishings, the quality of the craftsmanship throughout is very impressive.

73   South Tidworth, St Mary

SU 235 477

Passing through the garrison town of Tidworth, the visitor will hardly be prepared for this complete mid-Victorian 'gem', as H S Goodhart-Rendel described the church. It stands by the road on the edge of the grounds of Tidworth House. Readers of Francis Brett Young's *Portrait of Clare* may recall the thinly disguised references to it.

John Johnson designed it for Sir John Kelk in 1878, the two having already been associated at the Alexandra Palace in North London. The thin spire is, to say the least, unusual. The stately interior, modelled on Sketton in North Yorkshire, is more harmonious, with its rich carving, elegant arcades and generous use of expensive materials.

74   Croome D'Abitot, St Mary Magdalen
SO 887 451

When the 6th Earl of Coventry decided to demolish his Jacobean house and build an elegant new house with a fine park, he took the opportunity to demolish the ancient church adjoining it and to erect a new one a few hundred yards away on the hill. The new church, completed in 1763, was designed by Capability Brown with Robert Adam responsible for its interior features. It is a perfect fantasy of the period, with elegant Gothick windows and plaster work, with its original font, pulpit communion rails, Commandments and Creed boards. The splendid monuments to the Coventry family were brought from the old church.

75　Evesham, St Lawrence
SP 037 436

St Lawrence's, with its tower and modest spire, the parish church of All Saints and the great Perpendicular Bell Tower of the Abbey, form a spectacular architectural group. To the east, beyond the shared churchyard, lawns stretch to the River Avon; to the north lies the Norman Abbey gateway; to the south-west is the 15th-century Almonry, now a museum.

Standing within the walls of the former Abbey, St Lawrence's is of Norman foundation, though as it appears now it is entirely Perpendicular. Internally this is due to the impressive restoration by Henry Eginton in 1836 after it fell into ruin in the 18th century.

The most remarkable feature of the exterior is the east wall of the chancel, which is completely filled by the great six-light window with elaborate tracery. The early 16th-century chantry chapel of St Clement has richly panelled arches internally and beautiful fan vaulting. The windows contain stained glass of many of the major glaziers of the last 150 years; particularly fine is the east window, dated 1882, by Thomas Willement. Eginton's continuous ceiling of the nave and chancel is panelled with moulded ribs, alternately large and small. Of the fittings, the Victorian tiles in the chancel are of excellent quality, as are the pulpit and details of the reredos.

76　Llanrothal, St John the Baptist
SO 471 185

Down a long cul-de-sac, in a remote situation appreciated by wildlife and its observers, stands the church of Llanrothal, within yards of the River Monnow and the Welsh border. This is as far as the Fund's writ runs. The nave has a 12th-century window, the east window is *c*.1300 and the beautiful south window *c*.1400, but the site may be considerably older, associated with the Celtic St Ridol.

The building was rescued from total ruin in 1921 and again in the 1950s by the Historic Churches Preservation Trust and the Friends of Friendless Churches. The nave was re-roofed by the Fund in 1988 to preserve the early nave walls.

77 Michaelchurch, St Michael
SO 522 257

Situated down a narrow lane (which the local authority resolutely refuses to signpost), beside a pond and often with an apparently amiable pony cropping the churchyard grass, this is an idyllic setting for a church which is probably unique in having a Roman altar facing the principal doorway. The inscription suggests that it was given by a Roman soldier, Beccicus, to 'the god of the three ways'. It was subsequently used as a stoup. But this is far from being the only claim to a visit by this deeply rural church near Ross-on-Wye.

Built in the 11th or 12th century, it was largely restored in the 13th, and a porch was added in the 17th century. The font, with tapering cylindrical bowl, is as old as the church. On all but the west wall there are remains of 13th-century painted decoration on plaster, and superimposed on these on the north and south walls are black-letter inscriptions from the 16th and 17th centuries. There is also an early 16th-century chancel screen.

78 Moreton Jeffries Church
SU 001 385

The church stands across a field at the end of a cul-de-sac, with a thin scatter of houses around it. It is a long low building constructed in stone, with a small slated bell-cote at the west end.

The vernacular appeal of the exterior applies also within except for the elaborately carved Jacobean pulpit with sounding-board which is considerably more sophisticated. The chancel roof is ascribed to the 17th century; one box-pew remains and older wood is incorporated in the benches. The 1860 Creed, Lord's Prayer and Commandment boards are of good quality.

79 Pendock Church
SO 817 337

Pendock church is a welcome feature in
the landscape to the traveller on the M50
Ross-on-Wye spur which passes directly
beneath it some five miles west of Tewkesbury. The church now stands remote
from its village but depressions in the
fields to the north indicate the site of
monastic buildings and point to its origin
as a chapel for a cell of Little Malvern
Priory.

This is a church of great charm. The nave
and chancel date from the late 12th
century and new windows were added in
the 14th when also the tower was built.
Surviving Norman features include the
chancel arch, the north and south doorways and the font. Among the many good
fittings are the north door, Jacobean communion rails, 16th-century pews and an
organ which may once have belonged to
Sir Edward Elgar.

80 Spetchley, All Saints
SO 895 539

Spetchley is a small village, four miles
east of Worcester, now separated from the
city by the M5 motorway. The church,
which adjoins Spetchley Park and its
gardens, is largely hidden by the trees,
one of which — an ancient yew in the
churchyard — dwarfs it.

It is a simple early-14th-century building,
with a west tower built within the west
end of the nave in the 17th century. A
large chapel, added in 1614 on the south
side of the chancel, contains an outstanding series of monuments to members of
the Berkeley family, the owners of the
Park. Centrally placed is the monument
to Sir Rowland Berkeley (d. 1611), consisting of a large alabaster tomb chest
with obelisks at each corner and effigies
under a semicircular vault carried on
Ionic pillars.

81   Stretford, St Cosmas and St Damian
SO 443 557

The church's unusual dedication is recorded by Dingley in the 17th century but the shrine to the Saints in the church is medieval. They are the patron saints of physicians and surgeons.

As unusual as the dedication is the broad span of the roof, which was constructed about 1540 to cover both naves and both chancels. The north wall is 12th-century and a new nave and chancel were added in the early 13th to what is now the north chapel and aisle. The whole building was lengthened to the east about 1325, possibly by Robert de la Bere whose monument is in the north chapel. The other rather later monument is probably that of Sir John de la Bere.

The massive timbers of the roof and the heavy screens are a fine monument to a people in a remote place who knew their craft and their materials.

82   Worcester, St Swithun
SO 851 549

Few churches in the country can equal St Swithun's as an example of early Georgian church architecture, little affected by subsequent changes in fashion.

It was built in 1734–6 by Edward and Thomas Woodward of Chipping Camden, who refaced the tower of the previous church on the site and reused part of its north wall. Inside and out it is a stylish and almost unaltered example of a church of its date, with the three-decker pulpit, tester and Mayor's pew standing out from a sea of box-pews. Over the tester is a pelican feeding her young and below this an anchor entwined by a snake, representing the steadfast church resisting the wiles of the devil, but conveying an oddly nautical message in this inland city.

The east elevation would not look amiss in Italy. Much of the glass is original, where it has escaped vandalism, and the six bells date from the 15th and 17th centuries. Above the furnishings is a plaster ceiling and at the west end a fine 18th-century organ on its gallery.

83 Wormsley, St Mary the Virgin
SO 427 478

This little church is 12th-century in origin on an even older site. The nave, font and south doorway are evidence of this and the bell-cote and one of the bells are 13th-century. This early origin is somewhat concealed by the 1866–7 restoration, even though the old stone was used.

The setting is appropriately attractive, in hilly country eight miles north-west of Hereford. In the churchyard, which is not in the Fund's care, are the table tombs of Richard Payne Knight and Thomas Andrew Knight. The former's writing helped to guide taste to the rugged country beloved of the Romantics (Dorothy Wordsworth records reading him at Grasmere), and the latter made a crucial contribution to the development of the cider apple.

84 Yatton Chapel
SO 626 304

The simplicity of this tiny church and its farmyard setting convey a strong sense of the remote and the romantic. This is reinforced by the 12th-century tympanum over the door, the gradually eroding shafts below, the agricultural floor and the largely unplastered walls. This holy place, wild but not savage, is just a little enchanted.

85 Yazor, St Mary the Virgin
SO 406 466

The church stands out beside the A480 a few miles north-west of Hereford. It was built in 1843–51 at the expense of Uvedale Price of Mongewell (the church there also being in the Fund's care) and of his son. The elder Price's interest in landscape is discernible in the churchyard. The architect was George Moore, probably a pupil of Edward Blore, but the spire and remarkable fittings were completed by the rector, the Reverend R L Freer, DD.

Outside and in, St Mary's is an idiosyncratic building. Wood for the fittings came from the estate; there is good quality stained glass and grisaille. Many of the monuments must have come from the old church, a field away. The sanctuary is a riot of colour and carving while the Gurney stove, centrally placed, seems almost to have liturgical significance.

HERTFORDSHIRE

86 Buckland, St Andrew
TL 359 339

Buckland is a small compact village on the chalk uplands between Royston and Buntingford on the busy A10 road. The church occupies the highest point, away from the main road. The chancel dates from about 1350, the tower about 1400 and the south aisle and south porch are 15th-century. There is a wealth of 14th- and 15th-century carved stonework – including corbels which supported the former rood screen – and there are fragments of medieval glass and 15th-century brasses. The fittings are of various dates in the 19th century, the pulpit being especially notable. The 15th-century south doorway retains its original wooden door complete with medieval framework.

87 Oxhey Chapel
TQ 113 934

One of the Fund's most delicious surprises, this flint and brick building redolent of the 17th century is squeezed between the 1953 church and its vicarage and surrounded by a late 1940s housing estate.

The chapel was built in 1612 by Sir James Altham, who held high office under Elizabeth I and James I. It acquired its present collegiate-style arrangements as a result of an 1897 restoration, carried out at the expense of Thomas Blackwell, the food manufacturer.

The superb reredos with its barley-sugar columns, the font, west doorway, roof, communion-rails and sanctuary paving are all 17th-century, as is the Altham monument. The Victorian furnishings complement the earlier work.

This gem is only a short journey from Euston, then five minutes' walk from Carpenders Park Station.

88 Stanstead Abbotts, St James
TL 399 111

The history of the village is closely linked with that of Rye House and the 1683 plot which sought to murder both Charles II and his brother, later James II.

The church dates from the 12th to the 16th centuries with a good 15th-century tower and timber porch. The delightfully unspoilt interior lovingly cared for, retains its 17th- and 18th-century furnishings, for a new church was built more centrally in 1881.

Among the fine series of monuments is one to Sir Edward Baesche, General Surveyor of Victuals for the Navy during much of the 16th century. There is old glass in the Baesche chapel, with texts on the wall. Above the plaster ceiling is a medieval king-post roof.

HUMBERSIDE

89 Barnetby-le-Wold, St Mary
TA 061 091

A few miles south of the soaring Humber bridge, this church is reached by an often-muddy path through a tunnel of vegetation and a fine churchyard. The name is Anglo-Saxon with the Danish 'by' at the end; and the hill-top site is said by tradition to have been used for pre-Christian worship. It feels like it.

There is early evidence of Christianity – a Saxon window in the south wall with a cat carved on it. The Saxon church, whose walls survive, was extended east in the 13th century. Probably the tower was once higher. Subsequently a north aisle was built – later demolished – and a large window inserted in the south wall. There are a medieval altar slab and the remains of a medieval screen. The chancel roof is dated 1660, the nave roof 1829. The delightful furnishings are early-19th-century. The famous Romanesque lead font is displayed at a local museum.

This is a church for those who prefer mystery to sanity, organic growth to Vitruvian rationalism.

90 Burringham, St John the Baptist
SE 833 090

The church almost nestles below the high bank of the River Trent, three miles south-west of Scunthorpe. One writes 'almost' because the churches of S S Teulon do not nestle. They stand out, wherever they are and this, built in 1856–7, is the strongest statement among his many country churches.

Its short but massive square tower with pyramidical roof and monumental interior has an all but fantastic boiler-house chimney at the north-west corner. Nave and apsidal chancel are wrapped in an unbuttressed wall. The tracery is in polychrome brick as is the decoration of the interior.

This is an extraordinary composition, both inside and out, and shows Teulon, who designed many of the simple yet solid furnishings, at his most dramatic and original.

91 Redbourne, St Andrew
SK 973 999

For some fifty years this village church, a little south of Brigg, was neglected and it came to the Fund in an appalling condition. This was all the more distressing because not only is it a distinguished building but it houses artefacts of national importance.

Unusually, the tower is nearly three times as high as the nave is long. Two-thirds of it are medieval – possibly with a very early core – with the top third added in about 1775. The interior is an unusual mix of medieval and Gothick, with idiosyncratic later additions. One regrets the disappearance of the furnishings as provided by the actress Harriot Mellon (wife first to the banker Thomas Coutts, then to the 9th Duke of St Albans), but the ornamental plasterwork remains.

Pre-eminent among the fittings is the incised slab of Sir Gerald Sothill (1410) whose garment and armour show some unique features. In the east window is William Collins's depiction of the Opening of the Sixth Seal (c.1836) in painted glass, which was based on the painting by Francis Danby, and the aisle windows contain more of Collin's work. There are good monuments, particularly that to Harriot Mellon by Chantrey.

Condition in 1980.

KENT

92 Burham, St Mary
TQ 728 622

Standing by the Medway and on the pilgrims' route to Canterbury, St Mary's was the old parish church of Burham. But the village moved to higher ground, built itself a new church in the 19th century (now demolished) and left St Mary's high and dry in the metaphorical sense and low and damp in the physical.

Burham Old Church is a pattern-book for young students of architecture as north and south aisles were added to the original 12th-century structure and then pulled down – rather like an architectural concertina – leaving the evidence of what had happened clearly visible. The exterior has a fine mix of materials and there is a stocky ragstone west tower.

93 Capel, St Thomas à Becket
TQ 637 445

Capel is to be found east of the A20, a few miles south-east of Tonbridge. In outline and texture, this is a good example of a Wealden church, but it has national significance because of the 13th-century wall-paintings on the north wall, restored in 1967 by Mrs Eve Baker.

Much of the church dates from the 14th century but the tower appears to have been rebuilt after a fire in 1639. Vestry, chancel and south wall are 19th-century in their present form.

Archbishop Thomas à Becket is said to have preached under the yew tree, east of the church.

94 Capel-le-Ferne, St Mary the Virgin
TR 257 400

From this church, which stands almost on its own on bleak downland above Folkestone, one can almost see France. A Norman window with a little contemporary wall-painting in the reveal indicates the building's early origin. Its best known feature is a stone rood-screen consisting of three arches with, uniquely in England, an arched opening for the rood itself. There are a 13th-century piscina and a small brass of 1526.

95 Cooling, St James
TQ 756 759

This is the church of a small hamlet in the Hoo peninsula, north of Rochester, on the edge of the marshes. Cooling is otherwise notable for the remains of the castle, with its great gatehouse, built as a tower of refuge in 1385, a similar date to much of the church.

In the chancel is a striking scheme of twelve arches, sedilia and piscina, all richly carved and dating from about 1260. Old woodwork includes the south door, some early oak benches and part of the nave roof. Even the Victorian vestry is unusual for its walls inside are covered with thousands of cockle shells.

The church is especially impressive from the south-west, with walls of local ragstone, banded with knapped flints at the base of the tower. In the churchyard is a remarkable row of children's gravestones which may have inspired the opening pages of Charles Dickens's *Great Expectations*. On a misty day it would be no surprise to find Magwitch at one's elbow.

96 East Peckham, St Michael
TQ 661 522

The old church of this Kent village stands on a hill between Tonbridge and Maidstone, commanding fine views of the Medway valley and the Weald. It is of Norman origin, though the piers and arches are manifestly 14th-century and the windows chiefly 15th. It consists of nave with a south aisle, chancel with a south chapel, west tower, vestry and Perpendicular south porch. Inside are fragments of ancient glass, a brass inscription bedded, most unusually, in cast iron, and a Royal Arms of George II.

There are two centuries of memorials to the Twysdens, a local landed family which more than once touched on the political and intellectual history of the country.

97 Higham, St Mary
TQ 716 742

Now remote from its village, the old church of Higham stands on the edge of the marshes of the Isle of Grain.

Two blocked 12th-century windows indicate a Norman origin but the church was significantly enlarged in the 14th century when a priory of Benedictine nuns was established nearby and the distinctive double church came into being. It is thought that the nuns may have used part of the church as their chapel, which would explain the near symmetrical arrangement of the two naves and two chancels.

The woodwork is especially memorable: a 15th-century chancel screen in its original position, a 14th-century pulpit and, by the same hand, the south door, which retains some of its old ironwork. The Victorian restoration added some good stained glass in the chancel.

98 Paddlesworth, St Benedict
TQ 684 621

Set slightly above the industry of the Medway valley and below the trees crowning the North Downs, this tiny church seems to be part of the great barns of the farm which surrounds it. Abandoned in 1678, it was not used for religious purposes for 250 years.

There is stone and flint work possibly from the Saxon period onwards in the south wall and the church's own internal fittings have been enriched by a gallery and other furniture from Holborough Court.

The two simple cells of nave and chancel give as good, and as rare, a feel as one is ever likely to get of a village place of worship, 900 years old.

99 Sandwich, St Mary
TR 329 584

It is believed that a convent was founded here in the 7th century, and this is thus the oldest church site in Sandwich, though nothing of the convent now survives. There are, however, substantial remains of a large Norman church which was sacked by the French in the late 14th century and repaired by Sir William Lovery and his wife Emma, who were buried under the canopy in the north wall of the aisle. Their church had a central tower and spire which, weakened by an earthquake in 1579, fell in 1668, destroying much of the building.

Following the example at Wingham, on the Canterbury road, it was decided to replace the north arcade with chestnut columns. The immense 46ft breadth of nave and south aisle was roofed in one span. It was 300 years before this courageous feat of timber construction had to be strengthened.

The bell-cote was built in 1718 and through the centuries monuments have been added as one would expect in a long-prosperous town. There are a 15th-century font, a medieval Peter's Pence Box and other fittings of interest, and one or two unexplained details like the recess on the north side of the chancel.

100 Sandwich, St Peter
TR 331 580

St Peter's central tower dominates the skyline of this Cinque Ports town. A previous tower, much decayed, fell in

Tom Paine was married here.

October 1661 and destroyed the south aisle. Despite this, St Peter's has something of the scale and lightness of Dutch church interiors of the Reformation, with its tall arcades and clear glass in most windows. The present tower with its brickwork and cupola shows the influence of refugees from the Low Countries, who settled in Sandwich in the 16th and 17th centuries and much enriched the town.

There are traces of Norman masonry at the west end. The nave and chancel are 13th-century, as is the lower part of the tower which survived the fall. In the 14th century the north aisle was made higher and wider, enclosing the clerestory windows above the nave arcade. There are three 14th-century tombs in the north wall and the porch is 15th-century. At the south-east corner is a vestry with a gable, again reflecting Dutch influence, and below it is an undercroft, probably 13th-century.

St Peter's is used every year for exhibitions and other purposes and is one of the Fund's churches which has found a new role in the life of its community.

101 West Stourmouth, All Saints
TR 256 628

West Stourmouth is along a by-road which leads down to the Little Stour, north of Wingham. Surrounded by trees, the church has a nave with aisles, 14th-century south porch, chancel and a

wooden bell-cote over the western bay of the nave supported by massive brick buttresses. The internal evidence of a blocked double splayed window suggests that the church is of pre-Conquest origin. It has a 12th-century south arcade, a slightly later north arcade and 13th-century chancel.

Built in flint (in part still rendered), ragstone rubble and brick – a highly picturesque combination – the building has undergone many vicissitudes and alterations, most dramatically on the north side where the aisle was truncated in height and the nave roof brought down over the aisle in a single sweep. Inside, the south arcade has vigorously carved capitals. The flooring is attractive – red square tiles in the nave with three interesting memorial stones, stone slabs in the porch and pretty red and yellow diamond tiles in the chancel. The stained glass includes some unusual and interesting examples of early 19th-century glass in the late Georgian pictorial manner.

LANCASHIRE

102 Blackburn, Holy Trinity
SD 688 284

Holy Trinity stands on Mount Pleasant, close to high-rise flats, behind Thwaites' brewery and a brisk five minute walk from the centre of the town.

Edmund Sharpe (1809–77) was the architect. He had a substantial practice, largely in the north, and became a well-known writer on architecture. Constructed in 1843–6, this is a handsome building outside and finer still inside, having a Cistercian austerity which became rarer as the century progressed.

The particular glory of the church is the ceiling which consists of a series of heraldic designs painted on wooden panels. There is no record of how they came there but they must be original. They commemorate the families who contributed to the construction of the church, with a huge Royal Arms over the crossing and various royal and episcopal emblems around it and over the sanctuary.

In the transepts and the sanctuary there are tall, thin windows of great elegance, with original glass.

103 Lancaster, St John the Evangelist
SD 478 619

Standing at the busy junction of North Road and Chapel Street, St John's dates from 1754. It was originally a chapel-of-ease to the Priory church up on the hill by the Castle and did not itself become a parish church until 1842.

There is no record of the architect of the main part of the church but the tower and spire of 1784 were added by Thomas Harrison, who was responsible for much of the work in this locality, including the reconstruction of Lancaster Castle.

The spire is the chief feature externally, being in the form of a circular Doric temple surmounted by a small fluted spirelet – an imposing local landmark. Inside, many of the original fittings remain, including the galleries reached by elegant staircases in front of the west windows, and most of the pews in the nave.

104 Pilling, St John the Baptist Old Church
SD 403 485

Pilling itself is something of an island. This strongly vernacular old church is a physical expression of the village's social separateness and was left virtually untouched by the Victorians when they built a new church nearby. The date 1717 is above the door, as is a stone recording the curacy of George Holden, compiler of the tide tables for nearby Morecambe Bay.

The building is relatively long and low, and the interior is a perfect Georgian liturgical arrangement but with the pulpit at the east end of the south side rather than in the middle. There are galleries to the west and north with benches and box-pews below. The roof was raised in 1813 to accommodate the north gallery. Above is a charming bell-cote.

It is uncommon for a building of such simplicity to survive at all, let alone survive without suffering from the bright ideas of subsequent generations. Happy in its isolation, Pilling keeps itself to itself.

105 Tarleton, St Mary
SD 457 201

In a large churchyard on the A565 about half-way between Preston and Southport is the 18th-century church of St Mary. The busy main road now separates the church from its village where another church was built in 1866.

Standing on the site of a medieval chapel which disappeared in the 16th century, St Mary's is an example of a small early Georgian chapel which happily retains many of its original fittings. The picturesque bell-cote stands above a vestigial tower, heightened in 1824 when a porch with vestry and vestibule was added. The walls are of hand-made bricks except for the tower and west gable. There is original glazing in the four round-headed windows on each side and extra touches of elegance are added by the intersecting tracery of the glazing bars in the windows and the apsidal east end.

Inside, there are simple box-pews at the east end, open benches at the west end and stone-flagged floors. An L-shaped gallery crosses the west end and extends half-way along the south side. The original pulpit has gone but the reading desk survives. The communion-rails are of oak and are probably original. Industrial archaeologists would draw attention to the fine stove.

LEICESTERSHIRE

106 Brentingby, St Mary Tower
SK 785 188

Only the tall, narrow and highly individual saddle-backed tower and spire of this church are vested in the Fund, the rest of the building having been converted into a house. It is 14th-century, of ironstone with limestone dressings, and typical of the high-quality architecture of the period to be found in this part of the country.

107 Burley, Holy Cross
SK 883 103

Burley, Holy Cross, stands deferentially beside the Baroque grandeur of Burley on the Hill, umbilically connected to this big house by a passage which formed part of J L Pearson's restoration in 1868–70.

The restoration was so thorough that it can almost be called a Pearson church – though the building is none the worse for that – but actually the arcades are medieval, as is the font. The tower, with its impressive carvings and long belfry windows, is 14th-century and contains an important clock by Joseph Knibb, dated 1678. There is a Chantrey monument of 1820 to Lady Charlotte Finch, governess to the children of George III.

This remains a village church, unusually for a medieval building close to a big house. The monuments of the family next door do not dominate it and Pearson's strong, intelligent restoration sits well with the medieval work.

108 Leicester, All Saints
SK 583 048

This large inner city church stands on the main road to the north-west. It makes a considerable contribution to the townscape when viewed from the south, particularly the restored 17th-century clock on the south aisle wall and the housing for its jacks – now unfortunately stolen.

The tower stands at the north-east corner of the north aisle, with evidence to suggest that it might have been originally free-standing. The fabric dates from the 12th to the 19th centuries and has fine medieval roofs to both aisles. In strong contrast, the low, hard, red-brick chancel dates from a rebuilding in 1829. The thorough 19th-century work removed almost every trace of the extensive work to fabric and to fittings carried out during the 18th century. The large 13th-century font with its profusion of carving is outstanding.

109 Stretton-en-le-Field, St Michael
SK 304 119

Here is the epitome of an idealised version of a long-past rural England. Situated in gently rolling wooded country, the slender spire rises above the trees, close to the point where the counties of Derbyshire, Leicestershire, Staffordshire and Warwickshire meet, with the earthworks of former settlements a few yards to the north and, from earlier times, the traces of the Roman road which gives the scattered village its descriptive name.

Time has stood still here. The church retains its late 18th-century box-pews and other fittings in a fabric which had already been shorn of its south aisle. Little work was done in the 19th century so we have the relatively uncommon survival of a medieval church, patched up in the 18th century. The notable timber chancel arch, lined out to resemble squared ashlar, is of this date.

110 Withcote Chapel
SK 796 058

Set in charming, rolling country southwest of Oakham, this still looks like what it was intended to be – a private chapel to the house next door.

Constructed in the very first years of the 16th century, the chapel was altered – and entirely remodelled within – during the 18th. The date on the rainwater heads is 1744. The external alterations were unusually faithful to Gothic for that date.

Inside, the impression is firmly 18th-century, with a beautifully designed reredos, pews arranged as in a college, and a separate area at the west end for singers or the family. One of the elegant monuments incorporated in the reredos is to Matthew Johnson who built the Hall, having bought the estate from the poet, Lord Rochester.

The windows contain highly important stained-glass figures of 1536–7 – there is a heraldic reference to Jane Seymour, briefly Queen at the time. They have been attributed to Galeon Hone, the King's

Glazier, who also worked at King's College, Cambridge. The tall figures of apostles and prophets have been damaged over the years but most of the work remains. It makes a rare jewel-case of this small chapel.

LINCOLNSHIRE

111   Burwell, St Michael
TF 356 797

Partly shrouded in trees, the church of St Michael stands six miles south of Louth in the village of Burwell which lies in a fold of the Wolds. A steep path leads to the church between rows of yew and box.

The building is largely of greensand, with brick for the top courses of the nave walls and part of the top stage of the tower.

The most prominent feature is the chancel arch, a high-quality example of Norman work with carved capitals. The walls show evidence of alteration over the centuries and there was once a south aisle. The north wall is windowless and there is a possibility of former monastic buildings on this side. The fittings include a 17th-century pulpit and a series of monuments dating from the late 17th to the early 19th centuries. Carved angels, more typical of East Anglia, are fixed to the ceiling of the tower, probably survivors from an earlier nave roof.

112   Buslingthorpe, St Michael
TF 079 852

The unassuming exterior of this church, set in gently rolling country three miles south of Market Rasen, belies the treasures within. Approached from the west, its medieval tower, built in receding stages of the local Walesby stone and limestone blocks, stands framed by the large trees surrounding the part-moated farm to the east. The church and the few houses form part of a deserted medieval village site.

The main body of the church was rebuilt in 1835 to the designs of the local antiquarian, E J Willson, best remembered for his fine organ case in Lincoln Cathedral. The treasures here are two 14th-century monuments to the de Buslingthorpe family: an effigy on a tomb chest and a celebrated brass.

113   Clixby, All Hallows
TA 103 043

Three miles north of Caistor in the tiny village of Clixby is this residual chancel of a 13th-century church. It was in a ruinous condition until 1889, when it was restored and a west porch added by Hodgson Fowler. In the floor is set a 14th-century slab with an incised cross and chalice and the remains of a Lombardic inscription to Robert Blanchard, priest. The fine 15th-century font comes from Low Toynton and the pews from Miningsby. The base and lower part of the churchyard cross are medieval. This little church evokes holiness and has the qualities of a shrine.

In 1902.

114   Goltho, St George
TF 116 775

All that remains of the old village of Goltho is the church which stands alone just south of the A158 as you leave Wragby for Lincoln, and sheltered by a clump of trees. The great house of the Grantham family and its dependent village which once stood nearby, have long gone, and the sites have been the subject of extensive archeological research in recent years. On a clear day, Lincoln Cathedral, nearly ten miles to the west, is visible from the churchyard. The walls of this humble church are entirely of brick and therefore a great rarity in this part of the country. The chancel dates from the 18th century and most of the fittings are contemporary, including the pedimented altar-piece, the communion-rails, panelling and the two box-pews.

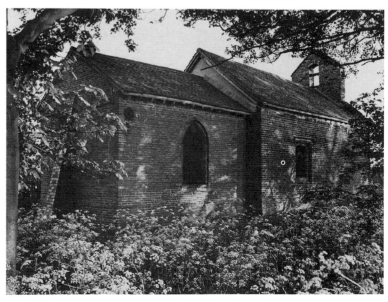

115 Great Steeping, All Saints Old Church

Situated in the marshland, three miles south-east of Spilsby, this small church stands sturdily on ancient foundations. It was built in 1748 of local greensand and brick. Before this 18th-century church was built there was a chancel, as is shown by the blocked arch in the east wall. A pleasant essay in a classical vernacular style, the church is now isolated from the village and is surrounded by a complex and undisturbed medieval field system, revealed by aerial photography.

116 Haceby, St Margaret (also known as St Barbara)
TF 030 361

Remotely situated on the sparsely populated uplands between Grantham and the Fens, all the main stages of medieval English architecture are to be found in this small but lovely church which has an enduring air of self-confidence. The lower part of the tower, the original nave walls and the chancel arch are Norman, the chancel is Early English, the top of the tower Decorated and the clerestory and south arcade are Perpendicular. Above the chancel arch are the Royal Arms of Queen Anne – a rarity, especially when, as here, it is painted on top of a medieval Doom.

Here the age of reason sits uneasily on a more instinctive albeit superstitious time.

117 Haltham-on-Bain, St Benedict
TF 246 638

Haltham is a small village on the road between Horncastle and Coningsby, the church standing by a green lane at one end. It has no tower but instead a quaint, low bell-cote above the west wall supported on timber posts inside the church. The timber boarding has inscriptions and a Carolean Royal Arms.

The inner south doorway is surmounted by a strange, almost barbaric, Norman tympanum under a roll-moulded arch. The outstanding feature is the lovely four-light Decorated window in the east wall; above the main lights there is an attractive composition of flowing tracery in a leaf-like design. A graceful 13th-century arcade of three bays separates the north aisle from the nave. The 17th-century pulpit is in the south-east corner and the pews face it; some have their original ends with curved elbow rests and lozenge-shaped poppyheads. The 15th-century chancel screen survives in multi-lated form, and the aisle screen is of unusual design not found elsewhere in the county, later adapted to form an L-shaped family pew.

This rarely visited church, only yards from a main road, richly rewards those who can bring themselves to stop for a few minutes.

118 Haugham, All Saints

Four miles south of Louth, Haugham church dates from 1837–40 and successfully echoes the outlines of Louth parish church, its spire having – in miniature – pinnacles, flying buttresses and crockets. Designed by W A Nicholson, it replaced a previous church on the site, of which some memorial slabs and the font have survived. When repairing the spire, the builders reported that they could see the shadow of Haugham medieval village in the surrounding cornfields. To the south the greensand tower of Burwell, another Fund church, can be seen.

All the fittings, apart from the glass of one window, date from 1840, the seating being a late survival of the Georgian manner. The arrangement of pews at Farndish, Bedfordshire, offers an interesting parallel of similar date. The style and date of the painted glass, especially that of the east window, is close to the outstanding series of aisle windows at Redbourne in South Humberside.

119 Kingerby, St Peter
TF 057 929

Kingerby lies five miles from Market Rasen. Though it is now tiny in population, the fields yield evidence of almost continuous occupation from Roman times. The remote setting of the church in leafy countryside is most attractive. From the east its tower rises out of the fields behind that of Kirkby-cum-Osgodby church.

There is a west tower, rising in tapering stages of decreasing size, which might date from the 11th century. The nave, south aisle, south porch and chancel date mainly from the 13th and 14th centuries and are built largely of the local Walesby stone. Arcading in the north wall of the nave gives evidence of a former north aisle.

Of special interest are the early 17th-century timbers of the nave roof; two recumbent effigies of knights on tomb chests and one deeply incised slab of a knight all dating from the 14th century, which commemorate the Disney family; and medieval glass depicting the Crucifixion, St Catherine and St Cecilia.

120 Normanby-by-Spital, St Peter
TF 002 882

This small village church, eleven miles north of Lincoln, contains early 12th-century to 15th-century work of good quality. The limestone arcades are particularly fine and the tower is sturdy and handsome. Foundations of a former apse are visible and further research may show that the church is of earlier date than the 12th century.

121   Normanton, St Nicholas
SK 948 463

Seven miles north of Grantham, the
church of St Nicholas at first glance from
north or east appears to be Victorian.
Closer inspection reveals much earlier
origins. The Norman arches of the south
arcade are 12th-century, the north arcade
perhaps a century younger. The tower,
with its particularly lovely limestone
masonry, is 14th-century and has a fine
contemporary door and wooden chest. A
clerestory was added in the 15th century.
Much of the medieval carving remains,
together with a 17th-century pulpit and
Royal Arms of 1820.

122   North Cockerington, St Mary
TF 367 914

This church has a history of unusual
complexity. Although a mile from the
village it served, St Mary's shares the
churchyard with Alvingham parish
church and lies within it, following en-
largement in 1923. It is believed to have
served the northern manor of North Cockerington before the Gilbertine Priory was
founded on an adjacent site in Alvingham
in 1154. Serving as the Priory's extra-
mural chapel until 1538, it was then
given parochial status after the dissolution of the Gilbertine Order. The ben-
efices remained separate until 1931 and
the parishes until 1981.

Most of the visible features of the church
date from the 13th and 14th centuries.
The tower was rebuilt in the early 19th
century; the box-pews and improving
texts over the arches date from that time.

Its unusual history and setting made
North Cockerington an obvious choice for
illustration in the Report of the Archbishops' Commission on Redundant
Churches in 1960 which led to the Pastoral Measure of 1968 through which the
Redundant Churches Fund was created.

123 Saltfleetby, All Saints
TF 455 905

Five miles north of Mablethorpe and distinguishable from afar by the Pisan lean of its tower, the church rises out of the marshland countryside. As the thin lancets in the tower and nave arcade show, the building is largely of the early 13th century, incorporating part of its Norman predecessor, traces of which can still be found, for instance in the south chapel. In the 15th century the top section of the tower and the windows on the north side were added. The detail of the stone carving of the windows – like that of the 14th-century reredos in the south aisle and of the font – is, as often in Lincolnshire, of very good quality. One or two details display the carver's wit.

The oak rood-screen is 15th-century; one pulpit is Jacobean, the other a little earlier. This and the reading desk were the gift of Oriel College, Oxford, and came from the College chapel.

This beautifully light, spacious and unspoilt church is lovingly cared for. It is a place of deep stillness and a worthy setting for its own furnishings and those that have come from Skidbrooke, Theddlethorpe, Miningsby and Oxford.

124 Skidbrooke, St Botolph
TF 439 932

Here is a characteristic Lincolnshire marshland church, standing by itself with hardly a habitation in sight, some eight miles north-east of Louth. A Grade-A building it is, as Henry Thorold has written, almost like a medieval Great Hall.

Consisting of a west tower, nave with north and south aisles, a now aisleless chancel and a south porch, it is impressive in its scale. Its general appearance is that of the 14th and 15th centuries but there are Early English features and the chancel arch is before 1200. The south arcade is astonishing with its octagonal waist-high bases of c.1400, shafts dating from a little later and 13th-century capitals, splendidly carved with stiff-leaf foliage.

Standing alone in the fields, it eloquently and hauntingly symbolises redundant churches everywhere.

125 South Somercotes, St Peter
TF 416 938

William White, the Victorian architect, wrote that St Peter's was known as the 'Queen of the Marsh'. One of the group of redundant churches north-east of Louth, it is easily identified, having one of the relatively few spires in this part of Lincolnshire.

The building is mainly 13th-century, with many windows inserted in the 15th century. There are two beautifully inscribed 1423 bells and the tower and spire probably do not date from much earlier. As often in this county, it is the carving, both of individual faces and of tracery, that is worth exploring. The 15th-century font is particularly noteworthy, with the instruments of the Passion carved on its eight faces. The woodwork too, is of good quality – a Perpendicular screen and communion rails of about 1730. The fittings are well worthy of this Queen of the Marsh.

fewer neighbours and one wonders where the Berties and Newcomens lived, whose monuments adorn church and church-yard.

The basic impression is of the 14th and 15th centuries, with a battlemented tower and parapets, but inside there are traces of a previous Norman building. The outside of the church has a colourful appearance as the local north Lincolnshire greensand is much patched with brick and Weldon stone.

The timberwork of the roof and screens is distinguished and there are some late-medieval pews. The two parclose screens probably date from about 1540 and have been compared with the Salkeld screen in Carlisle Cathedral. The grotesque faces have relatives in the windows of King's College, Cambridge.

126   Theddlethorpe, All Saints
TF 464 882

Some call this church the cathedral of the Lincolnshire Marsh. Like Ivychurch, Romney Marsh's cathedral, it is long and light, with little stained glass. It has even

The quality of the craftsmanship in this great marooned building makes it seem like a late-medieval precursor of the 'no expense spared' 19th-century buildings which occasionally come to the Fund, such as Yazor, Privett and South Tidworth.

127   Yarburgh, St John the Baptist
TF 351 931

Yarburgh is one of several small villages north-east of Louth, standing on the 25-feet contour line which marks the division between the Middle Marsh and the Outer Marsh.

The church dates from a rebuilding after a fire in 1405 and consists of a dominant west tower, nave with north aisle, and chancel. The south aisle was demolished in 1777 and the south arcade of the nave filled in, its present windows dating from 1854. The roofs and many of the fittings date from the 1854 restoration by James Fowler of Louth, when the medieval rood-screen was moved to the tower arch. The tower was underpinned in 1908.

Built in about 1450 in yellow Walesby stone, the tower is famed for its west doorway, in the spandrels of which are carved the Fall of Man, the Tree of Knowledge, Adam and Eve, the Devil, the Agnus Dei and the Cross of Christ — a remarkable statement of medieval thought and theology.

Inglesham, Wiltshire. *Christopher Dalton.*

Bungay, Suffolk. Chateaubriand, exiled by the French Revolution, lived here at this time; teaching French to young ladies and falling in love with the vicar's daughter. *Norfolk Museums Service (Norwich Castle Museum).*

Berwick Bassett, Wiltshire. By J Buckler 1803–11. There is now a small spire above the porch. *Wiltshire Archaeological and Natural History Society.*

South Cowton, North Yorkshire. *Kate Weaver.*

Edworth, Bedfordshire. *Christopher Dalton.*

Chandos Mausoleum. Little Stanmore, Greater London. Monument by Grinling Gibbons to the first Duke of Chandos, designed 1717. *Pitkin Pictorials Ltd.*

Covehithe, Suffolk, by Cornelius Varley. *Norfolk Museums Service (Norwich Castle Museum)*.

Uphill, Avon, *HTV West*.

Theddlethorpe, Lincolnshire, by John Piper. *By permission of R S Copestake.*

Saltfleetby, Lincolnshire, by John Piper. *By permission of Henry Thorold.*

Pilling, Lancashire. *Christopher Dalton.*

Tetbury, Gloucestershire. *Christopher Dalton.*

Michaelchurch, Hereford and Worcester. *Christopher Dalton.*

Stocklinch Ottersey, Somerset. *Christopher Dalton.*

GREATER LONDON

128   Little Stanmore, St Lawrence, Chandos Mausoleum
TL 168 922

In 1715 James Brydges, the creator of the great house known as Canons, who had become Earl of Carnarvon and was to become Duke of Chandos in 1719, pulled down the medieval church at Little Stanmore – except for the 16th-century west tower – and built a new church, the interior of which is one of the glories of English Baroque architecture.

To this he added in 1735, on the north side, the Chandos Mausoleum and anteroom, probably by James Gibbs. Its chief feature is a statue of the first Duke, dressed like a Roman and flanked by two of his three wives who kneel before him. It was probably designed by Grinling Gibbons about 1717. There is also a monument to the first wife (d. 1738) of the second Duke (by Henry Cheere, and to the first wife (d. 1768) of James Brydges who became the third Duke.

GREATER MANCHESTER

129   Bolton, All Saints
SD 714 108

Majestically, this 1880–81 brick masterpiece by Paley and Austin rises above row upon row of 19th-century terraced houses. The scale of the interior is impressive. It consists of an aisleless hall, its ceiling coved along the sides with a central vault, lit by large windows set high and with a bold west tower and small east apse. All the fittings are original and of oak.

The history of the church differs from many of similar date built by wealthy industrialists in the northern cities and towns, for in its early years it benefited from endowments set aside by its founder, the mill owner Thomas Greenhalgh.

The parish itself has never been wealthy, yet over the past fifty years the congregation has maintained the church in exemplary fashion.

130   Friarmere, St Thomas Old Church
SD 982 091

Generally known as the 'Heights Chapel', this is a well-known landmark, particularly to walkers. Built of local gritstone in the 18th century, it stands near the old Yorkshire and Lancashire border at Delph. The Roman road across the Pennines passes nearby.

The 19th-century fittings and decorations have been seriously damaged by vandals, damp and weather but enough remains to give an impression of what was once there. Its repair has been generously supported by Oldham Metropolitan Borough Council.

Visits in winter to this remote hillside setting are only for the very robust.

131   Heaton Norris, Christ Church Tower
SJ 889 908

All that remains of this fine Stockport church, built by William Hayley in 1846, is the tall west tower with recessed spire. It is a prominent feature of the townscape and a worthy companion to the parish church across the Mersey.

132 Warburton, St Werburgh Old Church
SJ 697 896

Experts have disagreed widely about the date of this building, some placing it among the most ancient churches in Cheshire, others doubting if any part is of pre-Reformation date. However old, the church's fascination is beyond doubt and its many visitors appreciate why it is so treasured.

St Worburgh consists of nave and chancel with aisle and a brick tower, placed oddly at the south-east end of the chancel. The interior is entirely of timber and the north side still largely timber-framed outside but, to make good the ravages of weather on the original framework and wattle and daub fillings, the restorers of 1645 filled in the south and west sides with stone. When the tower was rebuilt in brick in 1711, brick was also used for the chancel, south transept and vestry. The fittings are notable, especially the Jacobean communion rails and pulpit.

Warburton is an island of peace, close to the Manchester Ship Canal, the M6 Motorway and important industrial sites.

MERSEYSIDE

133 Toxteth, St James
SJ 352 891

This beleaguered church was built in 1774–5 by Cuthbert Bisbrowne, with a chancel added in 1900. It is a plain brick building with a west tower, situated just south-west of the Anglican cathedral.

The cast-iron columns supporting the gallery are Liverpool's oldest but those at the Fund's Christ Church, Macclesfield must rival them. In the east window is fine stained glass by Henry Holiday (1881).

Little else remains in this repeatedly vandalised building which has come to look like a fortress. As this is written, with glass all over the street and graffiti all over the walls, it is hard to believe, fervently as one would wish it, that St James's is a symbol of hope in the midst of Liverpool's despair.

Vandals have destroyed much of the interior.

NORFOLK

134   Barton Bendish, St Mary
TF 719 058

Barton Bendish is a tiny village some six miles east of Downham Market, yet, incredibly, there were once three churches here. The thatched-roofed St Mary's is the smaller of the two remaining, separated from St Andrew's by a road, a couple of fields and a few houses. St Andrew's is 12th-century and All Saints must have been of a similar date. St Mary's is 14th-century: its west tower fell in 1710. It is a wonderfully still, prayerful place.

One enters through a fine Norman west door, a relative rarity in Norfolk and a survival of the demolished All Saints. Inside is an unorthodox arrangement of old pews and benches; one has the date 1637 carved on it, and the holy table is dated 1633. There is a mural, possibly representing the sin of Pride, and various sad people are on the corbels outside – surely the one on the north-east gable was an architect.

135   Booton, St Michael the Archangel
TG 123 224

Booton church rides the cornfields of mid-Norfolk, its crazy twin towers uninhibited by the solid splendour of the great medieval towers of its neighbours, Cawston and Salle. It is a unique building, the product of one man's imagination.

The Reverend Whitwell Elwin, the rector, started rebuilding the medieval chancel in 1875 to console himself for the death of a son. Having spent three weeks visiting the English cathedrals and Temple Balsall in Warwickshire, in 1879 he turned to the nave. Elwin's genius has been to take accurate medieval features and arrange them in relationships of which no medieval builder would have dreamed. Thus the nave windows are copies of those at Temple Balsall, the north porch is taken from that at Burgh, the west window from St Stephen's Chapel, Westminster, and the doorway from Glastonbury.

The west front, facing Elwin's rectory, is the set piece with its three-stage square towers set diagonally at the corners with slender buttresses, blind arcading and pierced parapets with gabled battlements between crocketted corner pinnacles. A third tall pinnacle rises between the towers.

Fortunately the interior is as Elwin left it. The nave is dominated by the huge curved triangle above the chancel arch which is framed by the operatic oak angels of the hammerbeam roof. Contemporary fittings include a throne-like pulpit, the font, lectern, and a complete scheme of stained glass.

Lutyens' verdict on Booton was 'very naughty but built in the right spirit'.

136 Brandiston, St Nicholas
TG 142 214

With only a small and scattered population, Brandiston ten miles north-west of Norwich, is easily missed in a landscape dominated by the famous towers of Salle, Booton and Cawston churches. Brandiston tower offers the contrast of being very squat – an upper octagonal stage on a lower round stage, rebuilt at the beginning of this century and not rising above the roofs of nave and aisle.

The plan is unusual – the tower stands at the west end of the north aisle. The aisle was originally the nave, its chancel having gone by the 18th century. In the windows there is tracery of high quality, in a transitional style between Decorated and Perpendicular. The tracery lights retain medieval stained glass and later grisaille. Peeling grey paint on the walls inside the building shows that there was once decoration in a shade of light green, which would have enhanced the lightness created by the size of the windows.

During the 1985 repairs.

137 Buckenham, St Nicholas
TG 356 058

The peacefulness of this isolated building and the care taken by its few neighbours are a fine contrast to the vandalism and decay of the 1960s and 1970s. As indicated by its other name, Buckenham Ferry, the church lies close to the River Yare. It has an octagonal tower (not, as one might expect in this area, a round one), Norman in origin and 13th-century at belfry level. The walls are an attractive mixture of materials – flint, brick, stone and the remains of render. The windows are 14th- and 15th-century and there is a Norman doorway.

Inside are a 15th-century carved font, an east window by Samuel Yarrington (restored as far as possible, after vandalism, at the cost of local enthusiasts) and evidence of a very sympathetic 1841 restoration, especially in the woodwork and the moulded plaster ceilings.

138 Coston, St Michael
TG 062 062

Coston, nine miles west of Norwich, is little more than the Hall, the church and the former parsonage. Set back from the lane which runs between Kimberley and Runhall, the church is built chiefly of flint, the tower, nave and chancel forming an impressively complete example of the Early English style to which a small brick south porch was added in the 16th century. The exceptionally fine detailing of the 13th-century work is evident in the beautiful carved stone knots of the chancel-arch corbels and the piscina in the nave. The roof, with its massive tie beams, possibly dates from the 16th century and the pulpit, hexagonal with blank arcading and pendants, is early-17th-century.

The texture of both the exterior and interior – flint, stone, brick, pantiles, old render and plaster, all tempered by time – is a joy in itself. One hopes that decay will be so slow that nothing will need to be done to alter it.

139 East Ruston, St Mary
TG 364 287

The isolated 14th-century church of St Mary dominates the landscape from a high point along the busy road from Stalham to the North Sea Gas terminal buildings at Bacton and behind it in the distance rises the great tower of Happisburgh church.

The fame of this church rests in the carved 15th-century chancel screen with its lively lions and contemporary painted decoration. This includes representations of the Four Evangelists and the Four Latin Doctors on the panels of the north and south sides respectively. The octagonal medieval font, recut with considerable care in 1882, has representations of the symbols of the Evangelists on the faces of the bowl and frog-like demons round its base.

140 Feltwell, St Nicholas
TF 715 907

Feltwell is on the edge of the Fens, north-west of Brandon. Truncated fore and aft by a chancel demolished in 1862 and a west tower that fell in 1878, what remains is as broad as it is long, like a meeting-house. This impression is enhanced by the light pouring through clear glass and the 1830 brickwork of the north wall.

The porch is 15th-century and the elegant diaper-work in the clerestory of about the same date. The big Norman tower arch and the pilaster at the east end emphasise the church's early foundation. The north arcade is 12th-century, the south 13th.

As is the case with several of the Fund's churches, St Nicholas has been helped enormously by one person's energy and enthusiasm, first in saving the church, and then in caring for it.

141 Gunton, St Andrew
TG 229 342

As one approaches in autumn, one-and-a-half classical columns peep through the leaves in Norfolk parkland. Is this a deserted plantation in the hillier parts of Georgia or a forgotten temple in Vallombrosa? It is in fact a Norfolk church designed by Robert Adam and completed in 1769. Moulded ceilings and walls – look at the roses tumbling down to the gallery front – fine furnishings (some dating from 1894 but the Royal Arms from 1715) and a firmly rational spirit make this one of the Fund's most unusual possessions. Seen at Harvest Festival, the fruit and other decorations seem to have descended from the mouldings, grown and coloured – one could not but wish that by some alchemy they might go back and return to us next year, a Norfolk Proserpine.

142   Hales, St Margaret
TM 384 962

St Margaret's stands on its own, east of
the A146, closer to Beccles than to Norwich. Known far and wide by reason of its
thatched roof and round tower, Hales
church is a largely unaltered fabric with
Norman arcading round the apse, a magnificent doorway of somewhat later date
to the north and a good one to the south
also. There are mural paintings, including
a St Christopher, the remains of a 15th-
century screen, a beautiful 15th-century
font, and bricks, memorial stones and
pammets on the floor. The trees, seen
through clear glass, swaying in the wind
all round, were damaged in the 1987 gale
but one hopes they will grow again.

143   Hockwold, St Peter
TF 725 880

St Peter's stands beside the B1112, close
to the Suffolk border. Built of flint, with
some old rendering still there, it has an
unspoiled look, verging on the pleasing
decay beloved of John Piper.

The church is tall and full of light which
pours through its big Decorated and Perpendicular windows. The splendid nave
roof dates from the 15th century with
angels blessing the worshippers below.
The 17th- and 18th-century bells hang in
a very remarkable early 14th-century
frame. A monument in the chancel is to
Cyrill Wyche, one of the first members of
the Royal Society. His wife had family
connections with the Borbach Chantry at
West Dean, Wiltshire, another Fund
church.

144 Islington, St Mary
TF 571 169

This cruciform church was built in that richest of all ecclesiastical belts, stretching from King's Lynn to Wisbech. Tilney All Saints lies across the road and in the same modern group of parishes are Wiggenhall St German, Wiggenhall St Mary the Virgin, Wiggenhall St Mary Magdalen and the ruined Wiggenhall St Peter. The main part of the fabric was built in the early 14th century but the sturdy west tower and porch date from the 15th. Only the tower and chancel are now roofed.

145 Moulton, St Mary
TG 403 067

Two-and-a-half miles along the twisty road south of Acle stands Moulton church, in open country, alone but for a farm and its outbuildings. Consisting of a round west tower of Norman date, with attractive conical tiled roof, and later nave and chancel in flint, the church has Tudor brickwork in the porch and Georgian brickwork in the chancel east wall.

Many of the windows date from the 18th to early 19th century.

There are remarkable 14th-century wall-paintings of scenes from the Acts of Mercy and a representation of St Christopher, also noteworthy 17th-century woodwork texts painted on canvas and a 13th-century font.

146 North Barningham, St Peter's
TG 151 372

The church sits on a hilltop, some four miles south of Sheringham. It looks 15th-century but has earlier features, particularly in the north aisle. There is an unusual 1621 monument to Margaret Pope but many of the fittings have come from elsewhere, the originals having been removed under faculty before the church came to the Fund.

The passage of time has faded the interior into a subtle blend of colours which could never be reproduced – drab on a very dull day, but with the slightest hint of light (and there is plenty in this exposed situation) a splendidly warm effect is created, providing a fitting background for the fine series of Palgrave monuments, the remarkable medieval floor design in the nave, the superb angels above the chancel step and the carving in the sanctuary.

147 Shimpling, St George
TM 156 826

The village is three miles north-east of Diss; its church stands amidst fields, apart from its village. This is essentially a beautifully proportioned vernacular building, sympathetically restored by E C Lee in 1867–74.

The uppermost stage of the tower is octagonal and dates from the 15th century (as do two of the bells and the bell frame) but the lower part is some 300 years older. There is a fine late-medieval nave roof, the chancel is 13th-century and the nave 14th, with traces of earlier work. In most windows there is old glass, including small areas of distinguished medieval glass. The octagonal 15th-century font has carved panels on every face.

This is an outstanding church – not grand but, once discovered, unforgettable.

148 Thurgarton, All Saints
TG 181 359

Isolated from centres of population, Thurgarton church stands in open country in North Norfolk. It dates mainly from the 14th century and consists of a broad and lofty nave, chancel, south porch, and a west vestry of 1924, occupying the position of the round tower which fell in 1882. There is evidence of an aisle on the north side of the chancel.

All Saints is built of the traditional materials of the area – flint with thatched roofs. The height and length of the church are reminiscent of a great barn, especially as the timbers of the roof are now revealed, allowing a delicate scent of thatch into the church. Noteworthy are the series of medieval benches in the nave, complete with their original carved ends. As successful as the west vestry in blending with the ancient fabric is the chancel screen of the turn of the present century – a tactful and slender essay visually essential to a medieval church of proportions such as are found here.

All Saints is extremely fortunate in its next-door neighbour, whose efforts help to keep the church feeling alive.

149 Walpole St Andrew, St Andrew
TF 501 176

Walpole St Andrew is some eight miles west of King's Lynn. Almost in the shadow of its famous neighbour, Walpole St Peter, half a mile away, this is a fine 15th-century Fenland church but on an older site where Roman as well as medieval remains have been found. It deserves a better fate than the neglect of recent years and the serious vandalism which took place in 1986.

St Andrew's has a sturdy brick west tower, with a cell or oratory at its foot, nave with aisles, clerestory and octagonal turrets at the east end and a chancel with some old benches. The Jacobean pulpit stands on a medieval base. A painting by Sebastiano Ricci, which at one time hung above it, is at present on loan to the Fitzwilliam Museum in Cambridge.

150 West Harling, All Saints
TL 973 852

All Saints is a geographically sequestered church, although the top of the tower can be seen from a road, above the conifers of Thetford Forest. Externally it is an agreeable mixture of flint, stone, render and brick. There are good carved faces, especially at the east end, and a fine old door which leads into a well-restored interior, containing brasses of 1440, 1479 and 1508, fragments of old stained glass, Flemish panels in the reredos and, in the chancel, a handsome bust of Richard Gipps by Joseph Wilton (1780). The roofs, pews and other furnishings are of high quality workmanship of about 1900. All Saints is always colourfully adorned with flowers.

151 West Walton, St Mary the Virgin Tower
TF 471 133

This huge and splendid tower, detached from its beautiful church, was built around 1240 of Barnack stone; the quality both of design and execution put it in a class apart from the towers of most churches, even in this area. It recalls work at the cathedrals of Ely or Lincoln, with its four stages of arches growing richer in ornament as they rise. In the belfry are five bells in an ancient oak frame.

98

152 Wiggenhall, St Mary the Virgin
TF 583 144

This Fenland church, some five miles west of King's Lynn, is remarkable for being entirely of one period, in the early Perpendicular style, apart from the Early English north and south doorways. With the exception of the north clerestory windows, which have intersecting tracery under four-centred heads, all the windows have panel tracery. Although the walls are mainly of local rubble with limestone dressing, this is one of the earliest churches to have considerable use of brick in its walls. New roofs were provided by G E Street in 1862 and 1870 but his restoration left untouched the uniformity of the early Perpendicular style.

The really memorable features of the church are, however, the marvellous 15th-century benches with their carved heads, the brass eagle lectern of 1518 and the Jacobean font cover. The set of thirty-eight benches is indeed a great treasure, as they are amongst the finest in the country. Each bench-end rises to a large poppy-head beneath which are niches containing carved figures. On either side are lesser figures, some human, some animal. At the east end of each aisle are parclose screens, that on the north side now providing an organ chamber (the instrument is of two manuals by Holdich), that on the south side a chapel which houses a large alabaster monument to Henry Kervile (d. 1634) and his wife. The base and dado of the rood screen survive and there are paintings of eight saints in separate panels.

NORTHAMPTONSHIRE

153 Aldwincle, All Saints
TL 011 815

This magnificent church, three miles north-east of Thrapston, was selected for comment and illustration by the Bridges Commission (1958–60), as being one of a number of country churches whose problems deserved special attention. Although effectively redundant for over a hundred years, the church was not neglected. Repairs in the 1950s enabled the fabric to survive until the procedures prescribed by the Pastoral Measure came into operation after 1968.

The church dates from the 13th to the 16th centuries. The Tudor limestone west tower, with its fine carvings round the string courses, and the 1489 Chambre chantry chapel are of exceptional quality. The few remaining fittings include 17th-century communion rails. That the fittings are so few is not a matter of regret — the tall nave and aisles, with an uncluttered interior, give this church a rare majesty.

Opposite All Saints is the former rectory, the birthplace of John Dryden.

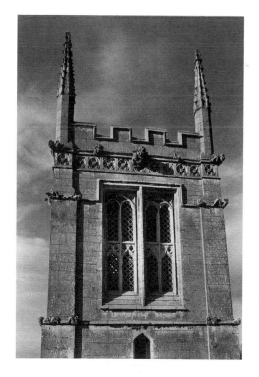

154 Blatherwycke, Holy Trinity
SP 974 957

The marvellous woodland setting of this church near Stamford is particularly memorable. Standing on a steep bank above a lake, close to the stables of the vanished seat of the Stafford and O'Brien families, the building possesses good quality work from almost every century from the 12th and has Collyweston stone-tiled roofs. Of the minor works carried out in the 1850s for the family and staff at the Hall, perhaps the best is the stained glass in the east window of the north chapel designed by J R Clayton of Clayton & Bell.

The tower is partly Norman, with a vigorously carved east window; the south doorway is also Norman. The nave and chancel are Early English and Decorated respectively and form an attractive contrast. Also Decorated are some of the windows, the carved frieze on the outside of the chancel, and a tomb cover with a floriated cross inside the church.

In addition to the Stafford and O'Brien monuments, there is an engaging memorial of 1650 by Nicholas Stone to the poet Thomas Randolph, who wrote to Anthony Stafford:

I will the country see
Where old simplicity
Though hid in gray
Doest look more gay
Than Foppery in plush and scarlet clad.
Farewell you city wits that are
Almost at civil war –
'Tis time that I grow wise, when all the
    world goes mad.

155 Deene, St Peter
SP 952 928

Deene is a small village some four miles from Corby, dominated by the great house and park of the Brudenell family.

A large building, it consists of a four-bay nave with north and south aisles, chancel with north and south chapels, west tower and spire, and south porch. A transept

was added to the south chapel in 1868–9. Although the church was extensively rebuilt by M D Wyatt in 1868–9 for the Countess of Cardigan, much of the walling, window tracery and carving throughout is medieval. The tower and broach spire are 13th-century and the west door, with its moulded label decorated with dogtooth, is work of high quality.

Inside, in contrast to the austerity of the nave and aisles, the chancel was sumptuously furnished and decorated by G F Bodley in 1890.

The south chapel and its transept contain monuments to the Brudenell family dating from 1531. The most remarkable is the marble sarcophagus to the Seventh Earl of Cardigan (1868) and his wife, its bronze panels showing scenes from the Crimean War. It is a magnum opus by Sir J E Boehm.

156 Holdenby, All Saints
SP 692 676

Wear stout boots for the long and frequently muddy approach. This is a church to savour and explore, and is at its best in springtime. Holdenby is on a small road north-west of Northampton. Here Christopher Hatton, a Lord Chancellor to Elizabeth I, was born. His construction of Holdenby House (afterwards partly demolished) involved the removal of the village, leaving behind only the church and some mounds.

Largely 14th-century, the church was much restored by Sir Gilbert Scott in 1867. The chancel had been rebuilt by Sir Henry Dryden of Canons Ashby in 1843–5. It is a fine building, made more appealing by the use of local ironstone. The west tower is tall and the aisles make the nave seem very broad. One most unusual feature is the series of seven large painted texts, almost certainly Elizabethan. There is much else, including a 15th-century memorial slab in alabaster and others from the 13th century and later. There are medieval stalls in the chancel.

The impressive 16th-century screen was brought from Holdenby House in about 1700. The chancel decoration owes much to Canon F H Sutton of Brant Broughton in Lincolnshire, as does the font cover. Much of the glass is by Clayton & Bell.

157 Preston Deanery, St Peter and St Paul
SP 788 556

On each side of the chancel arch there is a horizontal string-course with carvings which appear to be Viking in character, dating from the century before the Norman Conquest. The Norman builders of the chancel arch were clearly glad to use these carved stones, lengthening them to fit the space with similar stone decorated with chevrons.

The nave and western part of the chancel are Norman, as is the tower, with an original window in the east face and 14th-century windows in the others. The east window was inserted in 1808 but all but one of the others date from the 1620 restoration, after some years of neglect, by Sir Clement Edmonds, a clerk to the Privy Council of James I.

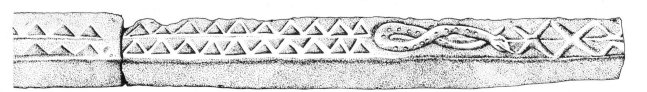

158 Upton, St Michael
SP 717 603

Set in trees beside the busy road from Northampton to the M1 and Daventry, St Michael's is an aisleless Norman building with many later windows added – so concealing its age to some extent – and a 14th-century tower inserted into the west end of the nave.

Some of its furnishings are on loan elsewhere but much remains, in particular a monument to James Harrington (d. 1677), the author of *Oceanae*. Naval historians will be drawn to the monument of a granddaughter of Sir Peter Gleane, Bt, who married first a Rodney, then an aunt of Nelson.

159 Wakerley, St John the Baptist
SP 956 992

This is a noble Northamptonshire church, set on a hillside above the Welland Valley, south-west of Stamford. Its magnificent tower was started in 1350 and the decorated spire is 15th-century, as is the east window. The nave has a clerestory and an aisle on each side, and there is a large north porch. The general impression given by the exterior is of the late Middle Ages.

Inside, the chancel arch tells a different, older story. Its zigzag pattern indicates a 12th-century origin and it rests on capitals that are beautifully carved and can stand comparison with the best work in England from around 1140. The robust font is 13th-century.

The nave roof was reconstructed in 1737–8 using old timbers resting on carved corbels, with figures on the main beam.

NORTHUMBERLAND

160 Bywell, St Andrew
NZ 048 614

This is one of two adjoining churches, the other being Bywell St Peter, marking the boundary between the baronies of Bolbeck and Baliol.

St Andrew's is distinguished by its fine Saxon tower at the west end, with characteristic windows and quoins. The nave and chancel appear to have been rebuilt in the 13th century, the nave on its original plan but the chancel lengthened; a south transept was added in the same or following century. In the walls are set a number of grave slabs with carved crosses, probably from the 13th century.

In the 19th century a north transept, north chapel and vestry were added in 1857 and further alterations were made to the sanctuary, probably as a result of a visit to Bywell Hall in 1871 by the artist, Walter Crane. The upper part of the east window is almost certainly by Henry Holiday.

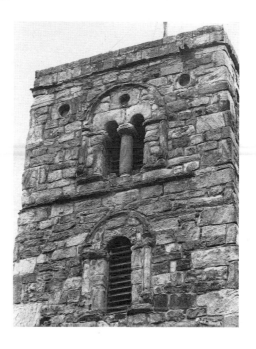

The two churches, down a cul-de-sac, with their graveyards and the adjoining park make an idyllic quiet place, little changed since Crane's visit.

161 Shotley, St Andrew
NZ 045 553

Standing 960 ft above sea level on Grey Mare Hill, this cruciform church was built in 1769 on a much older site and remodelled in 1892. It is approached across fields, remote from any centre of population and until recently the site of open-cast coal mining.

Of special interest is the Hopper mausoleum in the churchyard. Built in 1752, it is a square structure with statues in carved niches on each side. The Shotley branch of the Hopper family died out in 1818. The churchyard also contains many headstones attributed to John Graham Lough, who later worked in London.

NOTTINGHAMSHIRE

162   Elston Chapel
SK 763 483

Standing solitary on the edge of the village, Elston chapel is an astonishing survival. Its historical origin is obscure as it

was formerly attached not to Elston but to the adjoining parish of East Stoke.

Part of the small rubble-built fabric is Norman, with an impressive doorway of that period. Much else is 14th- or early 15th-century, including the fine square-headed windows, some of their tracery badly damaged but now reinstated. Early in the 19th century the chapel was refitted in a humble but decent manner with pine pews, a gallery etc., but retaining the 17th-century carved oak pulpit.

Regrettably vandals have destroyed or damaged many of the fittings and the Fund has a problem in deciding how much restoration to carry out if the very particular feel of the church is to be retained.

There is a connection with the Darwin family: Erasmus Darwin was born here in 1731.

163   Low Marnham, St Wilfrid
SK 694 806

Apart from the power stations which dominate the landscape of this part of Nottinghamshire, the broad plains of the

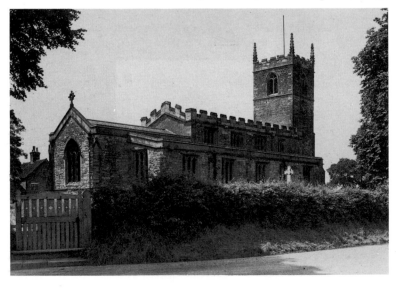

Trent Valley appear little touched by urban influences.

Low Marnham church (Low because it is 2 ft lower than High Marnham) appears similarly undisturbed. It presents an almost entirely Perpendicular appearance from outside. A porch was added in the last century possibly at the same time that the chancel was rebuilt.

Though in style and date they are similar, the arcades of the nave are, surprisingly, of widely different character: the north has low cylindrical pillars with circular capitals, while the south has taller pillars, octagonal in plan with detached shafts. All concur to present a delightfully proportioned interior. A series of wall monuments and memorial stones from 1733 to 1830 commemorates members of the Cartwright family.

164 Markham Clinton, Milton Mausoleum
SK 715 730

Visible from the Markham Moor round-about on the A1, this severe classical building with its strong cruciform shape and columned tower looks strangely out of place in the countryside. Designed by Sir Robert Smirke, it was erected by the 4th Duke of Newcastle in memory of his wife. It was intended to serve both as a mausoleum and chapel for the family and as a parish church for the community. Eventually none of these intentions was realised.

Vandalism and the weather have spoiled the interior but a fine screen remains and, in one of the transepts, Westmacott's monument to the Duchess has recently been returned from Clumber.

165 Saundby, St Martin of Tours
SK 785 879

Three miles west of Gainsborough, Saundby church is an example of an exceptionally sympathetic 19th-century restoration, to such an extent that it is difficult to tell where the medieval work ends and the Victorian restoration by the local architects Weatherley & Jones begins. They appear to have reproduced faithfully the Perpendicular low-pitched gables and embattled parapets of the late Middle Ages on the nave and chancel.

The three-stage west tower is dated 1504 by a stone set in its south wall. The north aisle seems to be a wholly 19th-century creation although it is likely that it was built on the medieval foundations of two chantry chapels.

Inside there is a complete cycle of Kempe glass, and in the chancel, an effigy of a knight in armour of the later 14th century and a monument of 1599.

Too long neglected, the church has lost many of its fittings and is altogether one of the saddest cases the Fund has had to handle.

Condition before vesting in 1986.

OXFORDSHIRE

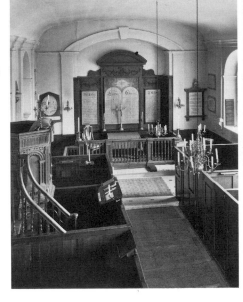

166 Chiselhampton, St Katherine
SU 593 992

Even in a county as rich in unrestored church interiors as Oxfordshire, Chiselhampton is outstanding for the beauty and completeness of its Georgian furnishings and liturgical arrangement.

The church was rebuilt on a fresh site in 1762–3 by Charles Peers of the adjoining Chiselhampton House, probably to the design of Samuel Dowbiggin. It has a strikingly white, unsophisticated, classical exterior, with a tall turret for the clock and bells reminiscent of those found on stable blocks of the period.

Apart from the 17th-century pulpit brought from the previous church, all the woodwork – including altar-piece, box-pews and gallery – is of the same date as the building and of excellent quality.

St Katherine's is one of the Fund churches which had a close link with John Betjeman, one of whose poems was written to raise money for a previous scheme of repairs.

167 Mongewell, St John the Bapti
SU 610 877

The building is to be found on the east bank of the River Thames in the grounds of Carmel College, a short distance from Newnham Murren church. It consists of a small apsidal chancel, Norman in origin, ruined nave walls and small west tower.

The church was restored in the late 18th century by Shute Barrington, a bishop of Llandaff, Salisbury and Durham, in turn, for a total of fifty-seven years, who lived at Mongewell House. After further restoration in 1880, the tower is now the main surviving feature of Barrington's work. In the chancel there are two unusually lively, if damaged, early-18th-century monuments.

Visitors are asked to avoid coming on Saturdays.

168 Newnham Murren, St Mary
SU 610 885

Though this flint church was built in the 12th and 13th centuries a zealous restoration in 1849 eradicated much of the Norman and Early English work but fortunately left the good woodwork, particularly the medieval roofs and 17th-century pulpit and communion table. The plain north doorway and the chancel arch retain their early Norman character. There is a hagioscope on the south side of the chancel arch. A south aisle was added to the original Norman church.

This is a very simple church in a charming setting close to the Thames. A short walk southwards down the path east of the church leads to Mongewell.

169 Nuneham Courtenay, All Saints Old Church
SU 542 983

The church stands in the grounds of Nuneham Park on a slope overlooking the east bank of the Thames between Abingdon and Oxford. Like many other churches of its date, its site was chosen so that it should be a landscape ornament, set in a landscape which Horace Walpole described in 1790 as 'the most beautiful in the world'. A distant view of the church can be gained from the former Great Western Railway as it crosses the Thames between Culham and Radley.

Built in a Roman style to the design of the first Lord Harcourt in 1764, assisted by James 'Athenian' Stuart, the church is a domed temple with a semicircular portico. It is one of the earliest examples to show the introduction of Greek mouldings by Stuart. It is lit by semicircular mullioned lunettes in Palladian style, high in the walls and dome. Inside, are Italian fittings of the 17th and 18th centuries introduced in 1880 and busts of members of the Harcourt family.

A 17th-century monument of high quality from the medieval church, demolished on the erection of this church, is housed in a small separate building in the churchyard. This, together with the churchyard itself, has also been vested in the Fund to ensure its preservation.

170 Wallingford, St Peter
SU 609 895

In the statutory list, this church is described as 'A Renaissance rebuild of 1769 with spire 1777 by Sir Robert Taylor in Batty Langley "Gothick"'. This does not do justice to the charming open spire which dominates the approach to the town from the east. It also looks particularly well from the road across the fields to Newnham Murren church. The nave has a coffered ceiling. The chancel and apse were added in 1904.

The church is a mecca for lawyers; Sir William Blackstone contributed heavily to its construction. His rather sinister tomb is in the nave and his memorial outside on the south wall.

SHROPSHIRE

171 Adderley, St Peter
SJ 660 398

Set in the rolling countryside and parkland on the borders of Shropshire, Cheshire and Staffordshire, this cruciform church dates mainly from the beginning of the 19th century. To that period belong the excellent cast-iron windows, made in the birthplace of the industrial revolution in the Severn Gorge twenty miles south.

The tower and nave, west of the crossing, remain in use, only the chancel and transepts being in the care of the Fund. The north transept is a survival from the previous church on the site and contains a remarkable 17th-century screen, roof and panelling with 19th-century heraldic glass. These are all associated with the Kilmorey family, as is perhaps the 14th-century brass of an abbot or a bishop in the chancel. The south transept is associated with the Corbets, for many centuries a prominent local family, who made possible the 19th-century restoration of Battlefield.

172 Battlefield, St Mary Magdalene
SJ 512 173

This large and dignified church stands in open countryside about three miles north of Shrewsbury. Save for the former vicarage and a cottage, there is no habitation near. The church was erected as a memorial to those killed in the battle of Shrewsbury (21 July 1403), including Hotspur; it was a collegiate institution served by a rector and chaplains until dissolved in 1547 when it became a parish church.

By the mid-18th century the building was partly ruined but it was saved and in 1861 a thorough Victorian restoration was carried out by S Pountney Smith, a distinguished local architect. The building is unusual, unmistakably collegiate in design and impressive in size. There are a five-bay chancel, four-bay nave of the same width and a three-stage west tower of c.1500. The exterior is embellished by crocketted pinnacles on the tower and chancel for which Pountney Smith was responsible.

The original windows are now filled with Victorian glass, much of it very lovely. They are chiefly Perpendicular but the westernmost bay of the chancel has three-light windows with reticulated tracery. At the east end is a large five-light window with panel tracery, surmounted on the outside by a statue of King Henry IV.

Most of the glass and furnishings date from the 1861 restoration as does the hammerbeam roof. A most unusual survival is a *pietà*, or carved representation in oak of the Virgin and the dead Christ in her arms: it is about 3 ft 6 in in height and probably dates from the mid-15th century.

173 Bridgnorth, St Leonard
SO 717 934

St Leonard's is an essential feature of the silhouette of Bridgnorth's 'High Town', viewed from across the Severn, with the parish church of St Mary Magdalene by Telford framing the view at the other end. At closer quarters, seen from the canyon of Church Street, the tower stands massive and mellow in the local pink sandstone in the oasis of its churchyard, surrounded by an oval of buildings, most of which have their own claims to charm the visitor.

It is a very large church, as wide (91 ft), with its two broad side aisles, as it is long. The medieval building (there are traces of a pre-Conquest building on the site), was chiefly destroyed in the Civil War in a great fire which swept through the whole of High Town. Despite repairs after the Restoration, by the 19th century the building was in a deplorable condition. In 1846 the chancel was restored and the western parts in 1860–1 when the north aisle was added. This later work was directed by William Slater, a partner of R C Carpenter, the architect of Lancing College Chapel. The octagonal Stackhouse Library was added in 1878.

Features of interest inside the church are the lierne vaulting of the tower space, forming an entrance porch at the southwest corner of the church, and the magnificent 17th-century roof of the nave.

The 19th-century furniture and fittings are of high quality, the font (carved by T Earp) being of interest for the subject matter of the carvings and the skilful use of different types of stone. The carved oak pulpit on a stone base was given in 1862 and there is a fine east window by Clayton & Bell.

174 Longford, Talbot Chapel
SJ 725 184

There is no village at Longford but its two churches lie about a mile-and-a-half from Newport, close to Longford Hall. The Talbot Chapel is the surviving south aisle of the medieval parish church, demolished in 1803. It remained as a place of worship till the new church now itself closed was built some ten yards away.

The architectural features of the tiny chapel reveal its 13th-century origin, with a wide blocked arch in the north wall showing where it formerly connected with the chancel or nave. The windows in the south wall are also blocked, presumably to accommodate the large wall monument of elaborate design to Thomas Talbot (d. 1686). The 'barley-sugar' columns with Corinthian capitals support a segmental pediment bearing a cartouche of arms. Draped curtains hang from a canopy and on the plinth stand two cherubs, one with a skull, the other with an hourglass. The original railings remain and the inscription includes a moving tribute to Thomas Talbot's widow (d. 1706).

The chapel also contains a 13th-century priest's memorial slab, the font from the 'new' church and two wall monuments to members of the Leake family.

It is the best Fund church for observing curlews.

175　Preston Gubbals, St Martin
SJ 492 196

In 1866 a large new church was added to the existing one, which became its south aisle, in this small village four miles north of Shrewsbury. That new church has now been demolished and the original building vested in the Fund; some of the materials have been reused in filling the arcade. A 17th-century font and an outstanding 14th-century effigial slab have survived all the vicissitudes.

176　Shrewsbury, St Mary
SJ 494 126

St Mary's stands in the heart of medieval Shrewsbury. King Edgar is believed to have founded it in about 970 on the site of a Saxon church. Later it became a College and it retained the dignity of a Royal Peculiar until the 19th century. About 1150 a large cruciform Norman church was built but in the same century there were considerable enlargements in the Early English style: the aisles were thrown out, the chancel extended, the south porch added. Again in 1460–80 there was new work, the most striking being the erection of a fine spire on an enlarged tower; also the finely carved nave roof was constructed, the clerestorey inserted and the Trinity Chapel enriched by the prosperous Drapers Company.

By the Reformation, which dissolved the College, the building was in essence what we see today, though the inevitable Victorian restoration took place, which particularly affected the chancel. The glass, one of the great features of the church, came largely from elsewhere. The east window was inserted in 1792 and the continental glass in the nave and chancel from 1840 to 1850. The splendid Jesse window dominates the chancel (it came from the collapsed church of St Chad), most of it being 14th-century glass. In the chancel also are panels which illustrate the life of St Bernard, early 16th-century work brought from Germany; other windows contain Continental glass of quality and there is also notable work by David Evans, the early 19th-century Shrewsbury glazier.

Few parish churches can show such diversity of building style and beauty of contents, all on a grand scale, blended into a whole which is aesthetically pleasing and spiritually uplifting. It is the cathedral of the Fund.

What Celia Fiennes wrote in 1698 is still true: 'the spires of two of the churches stand high and appear eminent above the town'.

177 Upton Cressett, St Michael
SO 655 904

Upton Cressett is down a long cul-de-sac four miles west of Bridgnorth. The Shell Guide to Shropshire accurately noted that 'one of the quietest and most lonely of valleys leads to this remote and peaceful place.' The visitor who makes the journey will see a church that is basically Norman, as the noble chancel arch, south doorway and several windows will testify. Also Norman is the arcaded font and in the south chapel are traces of 13th-century wall-paintings. The pulpit is 17th-century.

A visit is particularly recommended when the snowdrops are out, but at any season the situation is lovely, close alongside the Hall with its Elizabethan gatehouse.

178 Wroxeter, St Andrew
ST 564 083

The Roman name for Wroxeter was Viroconium, the fourth largest town in Britain. A considerable sense of antiquity pervades the church, which by the Domesday Survey in 1086 was part of a collegiate establishment.

Entering the churchyard between Roman columns, a walk round the building reveals obvious signs of construction at different dates. The oldest part is the north wall of the nave, incorporating massive Roman blocks. In the south wall of the nave is set an Anglo-Saxon cross-shaft.

On going through the 19th-century porch, one is faced by a huge font, which is part of a Roman capital, and a fine 14th-century chest. Elsewhere 17th- and 18th-century work prevails: the rebuilt south aisle, box-pews, Jacobean pulpit and, in the chancel high above the nave, communion-rails and vestry.

The massive tower dates mainly from the 16th century with an earlier base. Round Norman arched windows remain in the chancel but most windows date from the 19th century as does much of the glass. There are some fine tablets, particularly one to the 1st Earl of Bradford (d. 1708) and three handsome table tombs, one commemorating Sir Thomas Bromley, a Chief Justice under Edward VI and Mary.

SOMERSET

179   Elworthy, St Martin of Tours
ST 082 352

Elworthy is a small hamlet in the Exmoor National Park on the narrow and twisting B3188 road between Wiveliscombe and Watchet. Tucked into the slope of a hill, the church is scarcely visible from the road.

The square tower, nave and chancel, built of roughly coursed sandstone and lias, date from the 13th and 14th centuries. The chancel was rebuilt in 1695, the east wall again in 1846.

The medieval and Jacobean woodwork was delicately restored in the last century. The screen across the chancel arch is a Victorian restoration though it incorporates some medieval details and a frieze with the delightful inscription 'O: LORD: PREPARE: OVR: ARTS: TO: PRAYE: AN: NO: 1632'. The font of Watchet marble in the Gothick style has an elaborate Victorian cover.

180   Emborough, The Blessed Virgin Mary
ST 612 513

With its prominent central tower, this church, which formerly served the tiny, scattered hamlet of Emborough, stands on a commanding site on a ridge of the Mendips, a mile from Chewton Mendip and nearly six from Wells.

The shape of the church and its site suggest a Saxon origin, although much of what we now see was constructed in a vernacular style in the early 18th century. The tower, which rises to a parapet with four elegant crocketted pinnacles at the corners, has a 13th-century base, the oldest surviving part of the church.

Inside, the pleasing barrel-shaped nave ceiling has at its east end a raised plaster frieze decorated with stars and suns, resting on a shallow cornice with a grapevine motif. Fittings, belonging to the 18th-century reconstruction, include a rustic oak gallery, communion rails and a hexagonal pulpit.

181 Hardington Bampfylde, St Mary
ST 743 526

Enfolded by a busy and noisy farm, this is none the less a peaceful place, three miles north of Frome, where one may find hop-bines festooning the walls after harvest festival.

This was a Norman church whose chancel arch was later partly rebuilt, quite sympathetically. The nave was rebuilt in the 14th century, as was the lowest stage of the tower, the other stages and the nave roof being added in the 15th. In the chancel the north wall remains from a 17th-century rebuilding, the rest being 1858–9. The font is Norman.

The Bampfylde family connection lasted for 400 years and their memorials are in the church. Sir Charles (d. 1823) earned considerable notoriety but we can afford to be kinder for we probably owe to him the delightful box-pews, pulpit and altar-rails. His illegitimate son was rector from 1814 to 1855 and for six years employed as curate Whitwell Elwin, later editor of the *Quarterly Review* and builder of the extraordinary Booton church in Norfolk, now also in the Fund's care.

182 Holcombe, St Andrew Old Church
ST 669 507

A maze of small lanes threads the four miles south from Radstock to the Old Church of Holcombe, which is a mile

from its village and situated in a valley with the great Abbey of Downside rising magnificently above it. The large churchyard contains some splendidly carved headstones and tombstones, including the grave of Captain Robert Falcon Scott of the Antarctic.

The Saxon church on the site was replaced by a Norman one which, in turn, was rebuilt later in the Middle Ages. There were further alterations in the 17th, 18th and early 19th centuries since when the church has been left unaltered.

Externally simple and unassuming, inside the nave retains its late Georgian arrangement of box-pews, pulpit with reading desk and west gallery. By contrast, the porch, which incorporates in its gable a much recut Norman arch, is a more sophisticated piece of antiquarianism. Inside and out, colour and texture give the church a special quality of stillness.

183 Northover, St Andrew
ST 524 232

Today Northover is virtually a northern suburb of Ilchester, separated from it by the River Yeo. Standing on a mound, the church occupies a site of outstanding archaeological importance, close to a large Roman cemetery beside the Fosse Way. The County Historian has suggested that the well-endowed church at Northover noted in the Domesday Survey was in all probability a minster church of the 9th century or earlier. It might have originated as a late Roman martyrium or similar structure, like the one recently identified at Wells which is also dedicated to St Andrew.

The present church is a simple building in Perpendicular style, restored in 1878 by Charles Benson, with a three-stage west tower, nave and chancel with small north and south transepts. There are a Jacobean pulpit, pews and lectern made up from old woodwork, and a reredos of particular interest.

Members of the Society for the Protection of Ancient Buildings inspect the repairs to the newly revealed medieval roof.

184 Seavington, St Mary
ST 403 149

Driving west on the old A303, after Seavington St Michael, the road bends and for a moment points the driver straight at the top of the tower of St Mary's; another bend takes him past, a small field's width away.

Originally 13th-century, the church was substantially altered in the 15th, 16th and 19th centuries. It has been necessary, for reasons of safety, to strip plaster from ceilings and walls, revealing in the nave remains of a 15th-century roof, traces of mural paintings, and, throughout, a more complicated history than expected.

185 Stocklinch Ottersey, St Mary the Virgin
ST 388 172

Delightfully set on a lightly-wooded hillside, the 'upper' church of the two in Stocklinch commands extensive views and is in itself an outstanding feature of the landscape. It almost grows out of the hill, with the local stone of its walls and typical Somerset tower.

It is mainly the work of the 13th and 14th centuries. There is a notable Decorated window in the south transept which also contains tombs and monuments to the Jeffreys family and their collaterals. The porch is wide and low. The font is Norman. Battlements, buttresses and window tracery all attest the joy of the maker shaping and carving in his natural medium.

186 Sutton Mallet Church
ST 373 369

Sutton Mallet was one of seven chapelries attached to Moorlynch, which historically belonged to the Abbot of Glastonbury.

Although the great Abbey is eight miles east of the village, it is still the presiding influence over this part of the moor.

By 1827 the medieval chapel was in poor repair and Richard Carver of Taunton, an architect whose work always has great charm – see for example Holy Trinity, Taunton and St Andrew's, Wiveliscombe – was employed to rebuild it.

On the very eve of the Gothic Revival, Carver produced a building entirely in the Georgian tradition with the typical arrangement of box-pews, pulpit with reading desk, and west gallery, which fittings survive intact. He reused the medieval east window in the small apse and remodelled the west tower to make it square, adding a Georgian parapet. From the earlier church there are two bells of 1607 and 1657.

187   Thurlbear, St Thomas
ST 265 211

A handsome 15th-century tower stands close to the road, built of the local grey limestone and embellished with dramatic gargoyles. Beyond are the nave walls, also late-Gothic in aspect. The chancel is hard to see, so unless one does what one ought and walks round the outside of the church first, one is quite unprepared for the inside.

The exterior of the nave and chancel is decent but unexciting, but the Norman interior is serene and eloquent, with two arcades of honey-coloured stone with delicately carved capitals. The east window looks Norman but is actually a Victorian guess at what preceded its Gothic predecessor. From the chancel turn back and look again at the beautifully proportioned nave.

In the tower is a rare ring of four 15th-century bells from the Exeter foundry.

188   Upton, St James
SS 982 295

Upton tower is an attractive feature of Exmoor National Park, found at the end of a long lane. It is almost all that remains of the medieval church which ceased to be used when a new church was built in 1861. Now only the lowest courses of the nave and chancel walls survive. The panel-traceried tower arch had been obscured for years by heavy undergrowth but can now be seen for the handsome building it is.

SUFFOLK

189   Akenham, St Mary
TM 147 489

The housing estates of outer Ipswich prowl and prowl around but Akenham church remains rural and remote. Like many of the lesser-known Suffolk churches, it is small and simple and never served anything but a hamlet. One Norman window remains in the north wall of the nave; other parts of the building date from later in the Middle Ages, including the flint tower on the south side which also serves as a porch. The brick south aisle was added in the 16th or 17th century. There is a fine font with window tracery round the bowl.

After suffering damage in the Second World War, the church was rescued and repaired by the Friends of Friendless Churches in 1960.

The churchyard, which remains in use, was the scene in the 1870s of the famous 'Akenham Burial Case'. The prolonged and bitter controversy, which attracted national interest, was over the burial in the churchyard of an unbaptised child of Nonconformist parents. It culminated in a High Court libel action and eventually led to the revision of the Burial Laws in 1880. The story is told in Ronald Fletcher's *In a Country Churchyard* (1978).

190   Badley, St Mary
TM 062 559

Badley lies a mile down a deeply rutted lane, just to the west of Needham Market. The earliest parts of this remote church are early-13th-century but most windows are from the 15th and the top of the tower is early-16th. The south side is unaltered since an etching made in 1841.

Inside is a complete 17th–18th century arrangement of pews incorporating medieval benches and fragments of screenwork; much of the panelling is also 17th-century. The oak is all silvery grey with age, an extraordinary ensemble.

There are many monuments and memorial slabs to the Poley family who intermarried with other 'Fund' families – a Brewse from Little Wenham and a Wentworth from Wentworth. Poleys still live nearby. Only the east window, by Frederick Preedy, is Victorian.

This is a place of great stillness, for meditation and prayers like few others in Suffolk, or anywhere, the surroundings are much as they always have been and the church is safely far from a road.

120

191 Bungay, St Mary
TM 337 898

St Mary's tall tower is the visual focus of the town from a distance but the church is separated from the Market Place, the natural centre of the town, by a row of houses backing onto the large churchyard with its interesting 18th- and 19th-century headstones. A short distance to the east, on the other side of Trinity Street, stands the much smaller church of Holy Trinity with its Norman round tower.

St Mary's was originally the parochial nave of the Benedictine nunnery church which was built about 1160. The present building contains elements of Decorated and Perpendicular work; the tower dates from the late 15th century. A serious fire in 1688 led to a comprehensive rebuilding programme in 1702 and there were restorations in 1865 and 1879. Eastwards runs a wall which may have formed part of the choir of the original church.

A feature of interest is the delicate cresting of the 15th-century parapet of the north aisle, much renewed in 1865 by R Drew (William Butterfield's nephew), and repaired again recently. The interior has been limewashed – the gift of a local benefactor.

192 Chilton, St Mary
TL 889 423

To the north-east of the old market town of Sudbury there is a new industrial estate and, a few hundred yards to the north, is St Mary's church. It stands in the middle of fields, the nearest buildings being now the warehouses of the estate. A footpath to the north leads to Chilton Hall, almost hidden in the trees, and away to the east lies Chilton Grange.

The church is mainly 15th-century, built of flint with stone dressings. The tower and the Crane chantry were added in the 16th century; both are of brick. There was a thorough restoration in the 1860s.

Surviving this restoration are the fine early-16th-century roofs of the chancel and the Crane chapel in which are three major family monuments, the most important being that to Sir Robert Crane (d. 1643) and his two wives.

193 Claydon, St Peter
TM 137 499

About four miles north-west of Ipswich, Claydon church stands on a commanding site overlooking the valley of the River Gipping and the A45 road.

It is a mainly medieval church, possibly with Saxon work in the north-west corner of the nave, which was remodelled and enlarged by the Reverend George Drury in 1862. Father Drury, who provided Father Ignatius and his eventually unsuccessful Benedictine community with their first home, employed the architect George Phipson. They extended the chancel and added transepts in the Decorated style. The liturgical arrangements may have been designed with the new 'monks' in mind.

Drury himself was responsible for the design of the stained glass in the east and west windows and it is said that he also carved some of the stonework. It was he who achieved notoriety as the priest at the centre of the Akenham Burial case. The surviving 19th-century fittings are all of high quality and bear the stamp of Drury's personality. Left derelict for far too long before being vested, much has regrettably been lost including some of the stained glass.

194 Covehithe, St Andrew
TM 523 818

The ancient church of Covehithe, once consisting of a Decorated west tower and Perpendicular nave, aisles and chancel, was reduced to a ruin in the Civil War and a small new church built inside the ruins in 1672. The noble flint and lime-stone tower, with its ancient stair, is a prominent landmark from far around and a haunt of pigeons who make its mainte-nance a problem. A favourite subject for artists over the centuries, one hopes that the rapidly encroaching sea will leave the tower and ruins of the old church to be enjoyed for a few more decades.

195 Ellough, All Saints
TM 443 866

The chancel, nave and tower of this hill-top church south of Beccles all date from the 14th century, the original south porch being added in 1602. There was a restoration by Butterfield in 1882 who was responsible for the east window and reredos.

Features of particular interest are: the octagonal font of 15th-century workmanship with a modern shaft, a brass of 1607 showing Margaret Chewt in an enormous head-dress, a superbly carved memorial stone of 1748 in the chancel, and the late-medieval cambered tie-beam roof with braces to the wall posts.

196 Icklingham, All Saints
TL 770 730

All Saints is the larger church of two in what today is barely a medium-sized village. Fifteen hundred years ago this was an important road junction and the village must have continued to prosper in the Middle Ages. By the late 19th century worship had come to be centred on St James's, so All Saints escaped restoration.

The walls of the nave are Norman but the church was largely and gloriously rebuilt in the 14th century. To this period belong the arcades, the tracery (especially the superb east window of the south aisle) and carving throughout the church, some of the stained glass, the font, the south door and the famous chest with its iron scroll-work which is at present to be seen at St James's. The floor tiles in the chancel are an unusually good example of medieval work. Some of the benches and the remains of the rood-screen are 15th-century; the altar rails, pulpit and family pew are 17th.

All Saints has been called a treasure-house of the traditional crafts of people who work in flint, stone, glass, timber and tiles, while its thatched roof demonstrates that the tradition lives. It is also very fine architecture.

197 Ipswich, St Mary Quay
TM 166 442

Situated near the docks, islanded by heavy traffic, St Mary's is one of twelve medieval churches in Ipswich. It was built between 1450 and 1550. Its 73-ft tower is a significant landmark, almost a forbidding one with the dark colour of its knapped flints. Being built during a relatively short period, there is an impressive unity of style, with handsome arcades and clerestory filling the building with light.

Within, the most remarkable feature is the wonderful double-hammerbeam roof over the nave. As so often in East Anglia, there are carved figures of apostles and other worthies, while the spandrels contain less formal images. There is a handsome octagonal 15th-century font. The brasses, including the excellent Flemish brass to the Pounder family, are in Christchurch Mansion Museum in Ipswich.

198 Little Wenham, St Lawrence
TM 081 392

Little Wenham stands isolated in the heart of they countryside, though only six miles from the centre of Ipswich. The church is on a knoll on the edge of a farmyard. On one side stands a long 16th-century timber-framed barn, while across the churchyard is the late-13th-century fortified hall.

The church is early-13th-century – apart from the later tower which has a Tudor brick top – and is an unspoilt fabric of flint walls and tiled roofs. At the east end are important wall-paintings with figures and arcading contemporary with the chancel and dating from about 1310, the faces blackened by the oxidisation of the paint. There is a good series of memorials to the Brewse family. Other features are the rubble-built base of the rood-screen, showing clearly the position of the medieval nave altars and good 17th- and 18th-century woodwork including the charming balustrades in the porch.

It is said that the church was saved from destruction in the 19th century by the refusal of one parishioner to concur with the wishes of his fellows to have it demolished. St Lawrence's stands as a fine memorial to this village Hampden.

199   Newton Green, All Saints
TL 920 413

A couple of miles outside Sudbury, the church is set back from the north side of the Colchester road. The main structure dates from the 14th century though the north door of the nave is a good example of Norman work, with two engaged columns and an arch of three orders above. The chancel remains in parish use for worship but the nave (including a good 15th-century pulpit), tower and south porch have been vested in the Fund. The north wall of the nave is extensively decorated with wall-paintings.

200   Rickinghall Superior, St Mary
TM 041 746

Rickinghall and Botesdale form one continuous village, built along the A143 road between Bury St Edmunds and Diss.

This upper church stands alone, above and to the south of the village. The chancel and the three-stage west tower are 14th-century, the nave and the south porch were rebuilt in the 15th century and the whole church restored in 1868. The walls are of rubble, faced with flint and dressed with a light-coloured limestone; the surfaces are patterned in small chequers.

The nave is the most distinguished part of the building and the stone 'bench' round the walls survives from medieval times.

201 Sapiston, St Andrew
TL 921 743

The chancel, nave and square west tower all date from the 14th century. The Norman south doorway, which is particularly distinguished, indicates an earlier origin; it has octagonal columns with cushion caps, each with a scratch dial, and an arch of two orders, each order being elaborately carved with curious ornament. The 13th-century font also testifies to a building older than most of the present construction. There are painted consecration crosses on the north and south walls.

Robert Bloomfield, author of *The Farmer's Boy* (1800), which sold 26,000 copies in three years, worked here on the farm of his relative William Austin who is buried in the churchyard.

Sapiston is seven miles south-east of Thetford. Isolated and approached across a long field, St Andrew's is the quintessential Fund church — but say so only softly for others would make the same claim.

202 South Elmham, All Saints
TM 330 828

The former parish of All Saints was probably the oldest of the ten parishes which formed the old township of South Elmham. Situated in the thinly populated countryside south of Bungay, the church stands at the end of a lane with the old moated Church Farm adjoining.

The most noticeable feature is the round tower, early Norman in origin, but much restored in the 19th century. When the church was being renovated in 1870, the fittings were reordered according to Evangelical precepts and these have remained unchanged during the past hundred years. The altar is narrowly circumscribed by the communion-rail. In the nave the pulpit, with its reading desk below, is set half-way down the north wall, facing inwards. The massive early-13th-century font, a few medieval pews and some old glass, are especially noteworthy.

The churchyard is cared for by the Suffolk Trust for Nature Conservation, and wild flowers abound in early summer.

203 Stanton, St John the Baptist
TL 966 735

Apart from the crow-stepped gable-end of the chancel, which bears the date of its rebuilding in 1616, the whole of this structure – west tower, nave, chancel – dates from the 14th century, but is now unfortunately roofless except for the tower, which contains an unusual and now empty medieval bell-frame (and a veritable plague of pigeons). Neighbours care lovingly for the grassed interior and the churchyard is an oasis of trees in unhedged farmland.

204 Sudbury, St Peter
TL 875 414

Standing squarely in the centre of Sudbury, behind the statue of Gainsborough – the town's most famous son – St Peter's is largely a 15th-century rebuilding of a much earlier structure, the noble tower dating from 1460–85. This fine town church consists of aisled nave and chancel and a two-storey south porch. Of particular note are the font, carved oak north and south doors, the screens and stone carvings. High on the north and south walls are handsomely executed oil paintings of Moses and Aaron by Robert Cardinal (c.1730).

Butterfield thoroughly restored the interior in 1854–8 and Bodley redecorated and refurnished the chancel in 1897 – two examples of excellent work by distinguished Victorian architects.

It seems sad that this, the most prominent church in Sudbury, should, of the town's three medieval churches, be the one to be closed.

205 Wordwell, All Saints
TI 828 720

All Saints lies beside the straight and busy B1106 road between Bury St Edmunds and Elveden; and the casual passer-by, at the end of a cold grey day in January, might dismiss it as just a text-book Victorian product. He would be wrong.

Both doors have carved Norman tympana, that over the south door being particularly fine, depicting two hounds in a forest, and there are vigorously carved hunting scenes on the fine series of medieval benches. The font is also Norman.

The porch and western bell-turret are by S S Teulon (1857) but it is thought, and not only by his admirers, that he was not responsible for the 1866 restoration which removed a 17th-century pulpit and other fittings which would have been admired today.

SURREY

206 Albury, St Peter and St Paul
TQ 063 479

The village of Albury has three churches. The ancient church, now vested in the Fund, stands in Albury Park near the great house which Henry Drummond transformed when he became the owner. Having become a member of the Catholic Apostolic Community, he built a church for them in 1840 and then, in 1842, a new parish church in Weston Street, perhaps to get the rector and his flock, now estranged, away from his door. This led in 1973 to the old church being declared redundant. The chancel had lost its roof and the space under the central tower was used as a chancel.

The tower was originally the Saxon chancel, heightened in about 1140, with an idiosyncratic shingled cupola added in the 18th century, the south chapel and aisle are 13th-century; the timbered porch 15th and the chancel 16th. The south chapel was converted into a mortuary chapel for the Drummond family and lavishly decorated by Pugin.

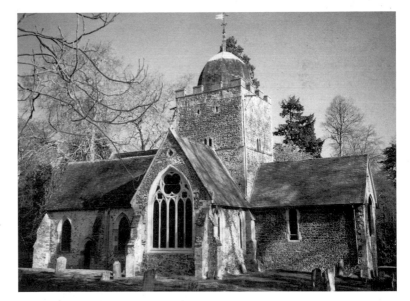

There is a fine brass of John Weston (d. 1440) and a 15th-century wall-painting of St Christopher. Uncluttered, with light pouring through the windows, the church shows the love and care its neighbours bestow upon it.

207   Esher, St George
TQ 139 646

St George's is a remarkable survival, a jumble of clunch and brick, roofed in stone and clay tiles. The nave and the chancel date from c.1540 and succeed an earlier church. Additions were made between 1724 and 1842 to accommodate the increasing population until the old church was superseded by a new in 1853. Since then St George's has been in intermittent use, but has survived unrestored and unscathed apart from the loss of box-pews in 1900 and the north gallery in 1934. Fortunately the three-decker pulpit and the gallery front were not taken down, so the complete interior can be easily imagined.

The Newcastle pew – a miniature aisle but on a mezzanine, with columns and a pediment like a house – was built to Vanbrugh's design. Worshippers have included Prince Leopold (later King of the Belgians) and Princess Charlotte, who lived at Claremont from 1816. Victoria, the future Queen, often visited 'her favourite uncle' there and near the end of her reign made a personal donation towards repairs to the church.

WEST SUSSEX

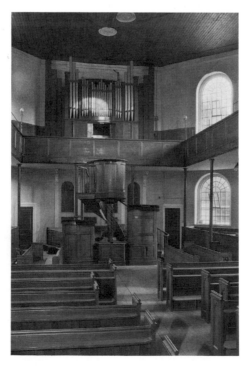

208   Chichester, St John the Evangelist
SU 864 046

This church was once described by John Betjeman as the most Evangelical on the south coast. It has a rare and impressive liturgical arrangement, with a very tall pulpit situated in front of the altar so that the preacher could see every member of his flock, whether in the galleries or below.

Built in 1812–3 by James Elmes, with a severe elegance rather gentler outside than in, the church is a stretched octagon of brick which was originally nearly white. Many of the fittings are contemporary with the building.

209 Tortington, St Mary Magdalene
TQ 003 050

Tortington village, near Arundel, is little more than a few cottages and a farm, behind which the church is tucked. The 12th-century church was once the parish church attached to Tortington Priory, founded in the 12th century for Canons of the Augustinian Order, and which was ruinous at the time of the Dissolution of the Monasteries.

Built of flint with dressings of Caen stone and chalk, the church consists of a nave with wooden west bell-cote, a south aisle and chancel, with north vestry. This south aisle was added in the 13th century, later taken down and finally rebuilt in 1860. Surprisingly the carved Norman south doorway, which has been moved at least three times since it was built, has survived remarkably well.

The small windows give the impression of a Norman church which has been little

altered, with a two-bay Early English south arcade. The most striking feature is the chancel arch with spirited carvings in Caen stone of a row of beakheads (unique in this county) alternating with grotesque faces or masks. Traces of colour show that the arch was originally polychrome.

210 Warminghurst, The Holy Sepulchre
TQ 117 169

The hilltop church of Warminghurst is approached by a narrow lane from Ashington, on the A24 road between Horsham and Worthing. Although mentioned in the Domesday Book, the present building dates largely from 1220 with later 13th-, 16th- and 17th-century additions and minor alterations.

Built of sandstone and other local materials, the church has a west bell-turret, north vestry and south porch or schoolroom. Its glory is the 18th-century interior; the nave is separated from the chancel by a triple-arched pine screen above which is a semi-circular plastered tympanum with the Royal Arms of Queen Anne painted on canvas, and on the east face an early-18th-century painted text. Along each side of the nave are box-pews, some with seats on three sides. The pulpit stands behind the clerk's desk on the south side.

Among the monuments is one in the chancel, which makes excellent use of various coloured marbles, to Elizabeth Butler (d. 1727), signed by Stanton and Horsnaile.

TYNE & WEAR

211   Low Elswick, St Stephen
NZ 232 633

Only the 1878 tower and spire have been
vested in the Fund, the remainder of the
church having been demolished in 1988.
It can be seen among the tower blocks
from the Tyne bridges on the north bank,
a little to the west of Newcastle city
centre. R J Johnson was the architect for
the whole church. Its austere lower
stages, exuberant belfry and slender spire
make it a worthy contributor to the city's
architectural delights.

212   Sunderland, Holy Trinity
NZ 406 572

Holy Trinity was built in 1718–19 with an
apse added in 1735, a new roof in 1803
and a west gallery of about the same date.
It is part of a small enclave of older
buildings near the Sunderland docks, and
would be a treasure anywhere.

It is a kind of provincial Wren building, a
large light space suitable for the burghers
of the prosperous port which Sunderland
then was. The unusual font was supplied
by Etty and Mansfield of York and William Etty is said, without clear evidence,
to have had a hand in the design of the
church.

At the west end are stalls for churchwar-
dens, sidesmen, overseers and constables;
behind them a narthex and large en-
trances, with ample room to meet. Much
of the 1719 furniture remains, together
with monuments to Jack Crawford, the
hero of Camperdown, and the Reverend
Robert Gray, also a hero in his ministry to
the victims of cholera and to the immig-
rants whom any seaport attracts.

WARWICKSHIRE

213 Billesley, All Saints
SP 148 568

Billesley church lies behind the Jacobean Hall (now a hotel) and is approached by a small avenue of lime trees. Church and Hall form the western extremity of the medieval village of Billesley Trussell, which has long since disappeared, though the lines of former buildings are clearly traceable.

Dating mostly from 1692, the church is an endearing small building in a rustic classical style. Of this date are the round-headed windows with their clear glazing, the communion rails, some of the other woodwork and the fireplace in the south transept, which was formerly the family pew, reserved for the occupants of the Hall. Much of the fabric of the church is medieval, the apse is assumed to be Norman.

Two sculptures found in the wall, must date from c.1140 and appear to be the products of the Herefordshire school, the most easterly example of their work.

Stratford-on-Avon being only three miles away, there is of course a Shakespeare connection: the playwright's granddaughter Elizabeth Nash was married here to John Barnard.

214 Brownsover, St Michael & All Angels
SP 508 774

Brownsover is a small hamlet north of Rugby, now isolated from new housing estates and the town itself by the link road to the M6. Near the church stands Brownsover Hall, designed by Sir George Gilbert Scott for Allesley Boughton-Leigh for whom he rebuilt the church in 1876, incorporating earlier features.

It is a small two-cell building in local stone without tower or bell-cote. The 19th-century ecclesiologist Matthew Bloxam, who is buried in the churchyard, described it in 1842 as 'one of the rudest structures of the 13th century I have ever met with, and from its very rudeness interesting'. It is to Scott's credit that his rebuilding lost none of that 'rudeness'.

Brownsover has its idiosyncratic collection of furnishings, some of continental origin, the best known being the organ case of 1660, originally built for St John's College, Cambridge.

215 Chadshunt, All Saints
SP 349 531

Long and low when first seen, All Saints gives an impression of massive strength and great simplicity. In the nave the east-ern end is 12th-century, the westward extension 14th, with an added clerestory in the 15th, providing the only north-side window.

The charming tower and its six bells are 17th-century. In about 1730 the present chancel was built, 18th-century elegance contrasting with the more homespun style in the nave. At the same time a north transept was constructed over a burial vault and many of the furnishings were installed. The font is Norman. In the transept are three windows of 16th-century Italian stained glass, brought here in 1855. The few monuments are of good quality, particularly that to Michael Askel (1731) by Robert Taylor, father of the architect.

Catch this church when the primroses are out, and with a low sun on the Hornton stone, and it creates an image one does not quickly forget.

216 Wolfhampcote, St Peter
SP 530 653

Three miles from Daventry, St Peter's almost sprawls across the fields, with humps of a deserted medieval village all around, two abandoned railways and a flourishing canal. This is one of several Fund churches which owes its survival to the Friends of Friendless Churches and the repairs they carried out, when neglect and vandalism had done serious damage to both fabric and fittings.

The oldest part, apart from the Norman font, is the 13th-century lower part of the tower. The nave, rebuilt later in that century, was completed in the next. The south aisle windows and the east window in the north chapel are 14th-century, the clerestory is 15th and the top of the tower is faintly dated 1690. The Hood mausoleum and window above are of 1848.

Inside are a 14th-century wooden screen, a group of late medieval oak benches, roofs with contributions from most cen-turies thereafter, 17th-century communion-rails and table, a Queen

Anne Royal Arms and a 1790 pulpit — all bathed in floods of light; one can almost hear Sarastro and his priests rejoicing in the discomfiture of the Queen of Night.

WILTSHIRE

217 Alton Priors, All Saints
SU 109 622

One of two churches in this small village, All Saints stands in a field just across a stream from St Mary's, Alton Barnes. Of the original Norman church, only the chancel arch remains. The rest of the church dates from late-medieval times except for the chancel, rebuilt in the 19th century but still containing Jacobean pews, unusually tall communion rails and a 1590 tomb. The west tower, of squared limestone, dominates its surroundings.

218 Berwick Bassett, St Nicholas
SU 098 736

Situated by a farmyard to the north of Avebury, this small church of 14th-century origin, built of sarsen stone and many other materials, consists of a Victorian low south tower, medieval nave and chancel, the latter rebuilt in brick at a later date but retaining the old window openings. There are an interesting 15th-century screen and 13th-century font.

219 Berwick St Leonard, St Leonard
ST 923 332

This little church, built of flint and Chilmark stone, blends delightfully with the surrounding domestic and agricultural buildings. It is 12th-century in origin, and a relief of the Lamb of God and a substantial amount of masonry survive from that time. The low tower contains a pretty porch. There is a handsome monument to George Howe of 1642.

The church was restored in 1859 at the expense of Alfred Morrison of Fonthill Gifford.

220 Chute Forest, St Mary
SU 309 521

Designed by J L Pearson in 1875, this is a fine example of Pearson's inventiveness on a low budget. Nave and aisles are spanned by a single roof, with tower and spire on the south side.

The church stands well in these very rural surroundings. Within and without, it is a pattern of well-proportioned architecture in brick, flint and tile, evidence of a distinguished architect taking pains over a relatively small commission. The church was erected at the expense of the Fowle family, whose mortal remains rest in the churchyard.

221 Everleigh, St Peter
SU 198 542

This was completely rebuilt on a new site in 1813 by Morlidge for the Ashley family, whose monuments are prominent therein. The church is a rare example of the transition from 'Gothick' to Gothic Revival and it contains its original fittings. The bells comprise a complete ring of six by James Wells of Aldbourne 1814.

Its main importance in architectural history is its iron-framed construction, revealed during repairs following serious water penetration over the years. The organ is by Gray and Davidson, 1844.

222 Fisherton Delamere, St Nicholas
SO 603 485

This delightful and well-concealed hamlet overlooks the Wylye valley, close to the intersection of the A303 and the A36. The church is typically Wiltshire with its chequer-work pattern of flint with stone dressings. A sturdy tower, to the south, also acts as porch and seems to peg the building into the sloping churchyard. It is medieval below but much altered – charmingly – above since Buckler drew it in the early 19th century.

In 1833 the broad nave was largely rebuilt, using a substantial amount of old stone particularly in the windows. The chancel is more purely medieval. To the north are a transept and small vestry. Between nave and chancel is a very fine screen of 1912 by F C Eden who was responsible for a number of other fittings.

223   Idmiston, All Saints
SU 197 374

Idmiston is one of several small villages in the Bourne valley, north-east of Salisbury, and the parish church is now the former chapel-of-ease in the neighbouring much larger village of Porton. Much of the building is late-14th-century and of some distinction, including the clerestory and the two-storey north porch with its steeply pitched roof and fine doorways. The nave arcades, given an effective striped appearance by the deliberate use of contrasting bands of stone, are late-13th-century. The base of the tower is Norman.

The whole building was heavily restored by J L Pearson and Ewan Christian in 1865–7. The shingled, pyramidal spire was built to replace a stone spire which had been removed in the 16th century. A remarkable feature of the church is the collection of medieval carvings, inside in the form of elegant corbel-heads and roof bosses, outside in the form of fearsome gargoyles.

Monuments include one of 1633 to Giles Rowback and several to members of the Bowle family. John Bowle, a vicar here (d. 1788), was nicknamed Don Bowle because he edited an edition of Don Quixote.

224   Inglesham, St John the Baptist
SU 205 984

The church stands on a slight mound just above the surrounding water meadows, at the end of a lane to the west of the A361 between Lechlade and Swindon. There is now no village of Inglesham, though there are the remains of a medieval settlement in the nearby meadows. The few parishioners live in houses and farms lying between the Thames and the little town of Highworth. It consists of a nave, with north and south aisles, chancel and south chapel with a bell-cote – small, befitting the size of the church – on the west gable.

The proportions of the nave suggest a Saxon origin and this is supported by the survival of a Saxon carving, representing the Virgin and Child and the Hand of God, which is now set in the wall of the south aisle. The remoteness of the church protected it from the heavy hands of 19th-century restorers, and a modest programme of repairs, carried out in 1888–9 by Micklethwaite under the eye of William Morris of nearby Kelmscott, did not disturb the original 13th-century building, which had received additions over the three centuries preceding the 19th-century work, nor its important fittings.

The woodwork of the roofs, of the 15th-century parclose screens, and of the 17th- and 18th-century pulpit and box-pews is nearly all original. Uneven floors and handsomely carved arcades make this as unspoilt an interior as any in England. Of great interest and importance are the wall-paintings, dating from the 13th and most later centuries. One scheme is laid on top of another and the Fund hopes to reveal the different schemes more clearly during the 1990s.

225 Leigh, All Saints Old Chancel
SU 058 928

The church, by J Buckler, before all but the chancel was removed to higher ground.

Standing alone in low-lying fields near the infant Thames above Cricklade, only the chancel remains of the old church of Leigh – pronounced 'lie' and often called 'The Leigh'. The local architect, C E Ponting, was persuaded, against his own advice, to remove the rest of the church to a drier and more convenient site in 1896–7.

Features of the old chancel, including the arches and windows, date from the 13th to 15th centuries. The east gable of the old nave was left standing and looks rather quaint, with Ponting's stone-roofed, lean-to porch stretching between the buttresses formed from the nave walls, to protect the great doors which now occupy the chancel arch. There are 17th-century texts painted on the walls and framed in designs of clouds and scrolls, providing a remarkable example of country Baroque.

226 Maddington, St Mary
SU 067 438

Shrewton, Maddington and Rollestone form virtually one large village lying in a sheltered valley in the middle of Salisbury Plain, a few miles west of Amesbury. Set in a shady churchyard, Maddington church lies at the top of a long footpath. It has a low west tower, a long nave, chancel and south transept, presumably for a family pew.

A few small fragments remain from the Norman church and there were additions and alterations in succeeding centuries, much being done in the 17th century. In 1853 the chancel was rebuilt and the whole church restored by T H Wyatt.

Both nave and chancel walls are faced with flint and sandstone chequerwork. The tower has lost its pinnacles and battlements which were removed for safety. Inside, over the tower arch, there is a large plaster cartouche of strapwork, enclosing the date 1637, which is said to refer to the erection of a now vanished gallery at the west end of the nave.

227 Old Dilton, St Mary
ST 859 490

Anyone who wishes to see characteristic church arrangements of the 18th century could not do better than visit Old Dilton. The interior is almost completely filled with box-pews, some of them built on the original medieval benches, and the three-decker pulpit and communion-rails also date from that time. There are a small west gallery and a larger north gallery with a fireplace.

The building itself, comprising nave, chancel, north aisle (partly used as a vestry), south porch and western turret with spirelet, dates from the 14th, 15th and 16th centuries. The removal of the 19th-century rendering has shown that the history of the fabric is more complex than had been thought. The church is in deep countryside, but travellers between Bristol and Southampton will often have seen it from the train that runs along the embankment just above it.

228 Orcheston, St George
SU 060 449

One of two medieval churches in a small village off the Devizes to Salisbury road, St George's was the Fund's two-hundredth acquisition. It is a charming church, pleasantly situated in a lush valley and seeming, as often in Wiltshire, to grow out of the ground, with its flint, local stone, hand-made tiles and chalky ashlar for the tower.

The north door is Norman and there are 13th-century windows in nave and chancel. The low tower with its fine panelled arch and the main windows are Perpendicular. The Royal Arms are dated 1636. Most of the fittings are Victorian.

229 Stratford Tony, St Mary and St Lawrence
SU 092 264

The approach to this church has few rivals, down a narrow lane, then on foot across a stream and up a steep bank. The church is just as idyllic – a variety of lichens on brick, stone and flint composing a perfect Wiltshire picture. The few houses are graciously spaced, suggesting community without too much propinquity.

The chancel is 14th-century and the tower partly of the 15th, but the font and piscina indicate an earlier foundation (a Roman road crossed the river near here). The nave was rebuilt, probably in the early 18th century. There are cut-down box-pews with attractive colonnaded tops which, with other furnishings and woodwork, make an unusual interior of great charm. One suspects the hand of C E Ponting or F C Eden but with no definite evidence.

230 Sutton Veny, St Leonard Old Church
ST 908 415

Three miles from Warminster, the old church lies down a long cul-de-sac to the south-east of the village. It was replaced in 1868 by a fine Pearson church and then used as a mortuary chapel; all around are old graves, some 17th-century.

The site, in the bottom of the Wylye valley, seems always to have encouraged subsidence, for the original church had to be largely rebuilt at the end of the 12th century and the story has been repeated frequently since. Of the building itself, only the chancel remains roofed; there are ruins of the nave, transepts and crossing.

The chancel walls have many simple, elegant memorials. There are benefaction boards, Creed, Lord's Prayer, a bier, a font and a bell; outside and in, all is lovingly cared for – this is a place of great peace and an absorbing lesson in local history.

231 West Dean Borbach Chantry
SU 255 274

This tiny and well-hidden building of flint and stone is all that now remains of the 14th-century parish church of West Dean. It was built by Robert de Borbach about 1333 as a chantry chapel on the south side of the church and hence has usually been known as the Borbach Chantry. A new parish church was built and the old church demolished, except for the chantry, in 1868.

Mr W J Evelyn then restored it as a mortuary chapel and moved into it a splendid series of family and other monuments from the body of the church. The large alabaster and marble monument to John Evelyn (d. 1627) shows effigies of husband and wife on their knees facing each other upon a base, against which are set figures of three sons and eight daughters in high relief. Equally notable is the large monument to Robert Pierrepoint (d. 1669), the grandfather of Lady Mary Wortley Montague, in grey and black marble, which is enclosed by wooden doors lined with painted latten and inscribed with an elegiac poem.

232 Wilton, St Mary Old Church
SU 097 313

This is what remains of the old church in the market-place, consisting only of a chancel and one bay of the nave, with the remains of the arcades and tower arch.

The chancel, with its delightful 18th-century ceiling, contains the memorial tablets to a number of vicars and other worthies, enough of them to enable the visitor to start to piece together the story of Wilton through two centuries. Here Bishop Bingham was consecrated in 1227, awaiting the completion of his cathedral at Salisbury.

143

233   Allerton Mauleverer, St Martin
SE 416 579

The Romanesque tower – not unlike the early Romanesque St Vorles at Chatillon-sur-Seine – is unusually but attractively placed just to the east of the transepts. This can make the church look like a big cat about to run its quarry down.

The Mauleverers were here for six hundred years (there is another Mauleverer brass in the Fund's church at Throapham in South Yorkshire) and founded the first church on the site. The present church was founded in 1745 by their successor, Richard Arundell, a Surveyor of the King's Works. The architect may have been James Paine or John Vardy. It owes its design in part to its parkland setting. It is not known what prompted the use of Romanesque but, especially in the west front, it is very impressive.

The style also reflects the liturgical practices of the mid-18th century – a preacher's church, with those who wished to make their communion going to the chancel through a gate. The fine hammerbeam roof, pulpit, pews and benches are all part of the 1745 design, as is the fine painting of Moses and Aaron above the chancel arch.

In the north transept are wooden effigies of late-13th- or early-14th-century Mauleverers, a brass of Sir John (d. 1400) and his wife; and a 1475 alabaster effigy of another Sir John and his wife Alyson. The Peckitt glass in the east window may contain a picture of the previous church.

234   Birdforth, St Mary
SE 486 758

Although many vehicles rush by this little church on the busy A19 trunk road between York and Teesside, few of their drivers notice either it or the hamlet. With rubble walls and pantiled roofs, the fabric consists only of nave, chancel and bell-cote – all simple but unspoilt and charming.

Originally Norman or pre-Conquest in date, the building was slightly altered in the Tudor period, judging from its style and from a coat of arms with the date 1585. Inside are appropriate fittings dating from the 16th to the 18th centuries.

235   Coverham, Holy Trinity
SE 104 864

Few churches can compare with
Coverham in its setting in the valley of
the River Cover in the Yorkshire Dales.

On an early Christian site, the church lies
low in the valley. The large, well-treed
churchyard has an interesting collection
of 17th-century and later monuments and
tomb-chests. To the south is the mill and
to the east the few surviving remains of
the Premonstratensian Coverham Abbey,
now picturesque features in a private garden.

In origin the present church is 13th-
century, with 14th- and 17th-century
additions, though the three-stage tower
belongs to the 16th. There was much
Victorian rebuilding, most of the fittings
dating from then, including some fine
armorial glass of 1840. An Anglo-Saxon
stone forms the lintel to the south door
and the most distinctive feature inside is
the early-14th-century four-bay south
arcade.

236   Cowthorpe, St Michael
SE 427 527

This village is just east of the A1, a little
north of Wetherby. Cowthorpe church
was built in 1456–68 by Bryan Roucliff, a
Baron of the Exchequer in the reign of
Henry VI. The military appearance of the
west tower reminds one of the Wars of the
Roses but its unusual construction may
be said to look forward several centuries.

Inside, all is harmony, as so often when a
building is all of one date. The famous
Easter sepulchre, the remains of the Roucliff brass, a bell, a superb (if heraldic)
font and more heraldry in the windows
were all the gifts of Roucliff and his wife.

Later centuries have added a porch, pretty altar-rails and unobtrusive 19th-
century furnishings. It remains Bryan and
Joan Roucliff's church.

237 Fylingdales, St Stephen Old Church
NZ 942 059

Built on a very old site in 1821–2 this church surely outdoes even Revelstoke in the grandeur of its situation above Robin Hood's Bay. Traces of the previous building emerged during the 1988 repairs. Externally as severe as the climate, with local herringbone tooling of the stonework, inside it is an unaltered example of a preaching church of its period. There are galleries to the north and west, the latter with an organ, box-pews below and, what matters most, a superb three-decker pulpit half-way along the south side.

The maiden's garlands which hung in the church for many years, have been conserved by the Museum and Art Gallery Service for Yorkshire and Humberside, with the help of a grant from the Council for the Care of Churches. Within and without there are memorials to the shipwrecked. Church and churchyard are pieces of history, rare in their forcefulness.

238 Lead, St Mary
SE 464 369

Well known to cyclists and ramblers, the church owes its survival to their love of this peaceful place. It stands in a wholly rural area between Leeds and Tadcaster, just off the B1217 road, with only two houses in sight. The field in which the chapel stands is full of low earthworks, which might be traces of the village destroyed during the battle of Towton (1461), in which the Yorkists of Edward IV destroyed the Lancastrians of Henry VI, thus bringing to an end the wearisome Wars of the Roses.

A simple and stoutly constructed single-cell building in local grey stone, with a bell-cote, the 14th-century chapel is filled with 18th-century woodwork and earlier open benches of elm. The floor incorporates a good collection of medieval coffin lids.

Repairs were carried out in 1784 and in 1932. More recently, archaeological investigation has revealed the lower courses of a former chancel, which have also been transferred to the Fund for their protection.

239 Roecliffe, St Mary
SE 375 660

Roecliffe parish lies in the valley of the River Ure, half a mile west of the A1, near Boroughbridge. St Mary's was designed in 1843 by Richard Hey Sharp, a Yorkshire architect, in the neo-Norman style then fashionable. Its place in the history of the development of 19th-century revivalist architecture is assured because of the unusual accuracy and conviction of Sharp's design, most notable in the great barrel vault.

The church is a simple rectangle to which a north vestry has been added. When the barrel vault showed signs of failure, only thirty years after the church was built, three massive buttresses were added to the north and south walls.

The architectural simplicity of the exterior is mirrored by that of the interior. It has not been recorded who amassed the furnishings but together they form a magnificent if idiosyncratic collection: the Jacobean pulpit, 17th-century communion table, the vestry door from York Minster (discarded by the Dean and Chapter after an earlier fire), and a series of carved panels in the vestry. Tiers of pews are ranged along the north, south and west walls in collegiate style.

240 South Cowton, St Mary
NZ 293 027

Apparently this church was built in about 1450, being completed in 1470 by Sir Richard Conyers, the site of whose castle is just to the south. His shield is to be seen in the 15th-century east window – indeed carvings abound. An earlier building may even have had a connection with St Cuthbert.

What we now have is a rather military-looking structure, with screen, choir stalls, wall-painting, a fine roof and consecration cross, all stemming from a century of remorseless civil war. In the chancel are the remains of three late 15th-century tomb-chests, possibly of Sir Christopher Boyton and his two wives.

This church seems to encapsulate what must have been an exceptionally uneasy time in English history, but also displays a remarkable standard of art and craftsmanship.

147

241 Stainburn, St Mary
SE 247 485

St Mary's retains its original Norman size – the church was never enlarged except by the construction of a porch, bell-cote and a vestry. It was built on some of the least good land in a parish where a living can never have been easy to gain. There are fine views across the Wharfe and to Great Alms Cliff. The site feels older than Christianity, not in a sinister way: just a natural place for worship.

A splendid Norman chancel arch is the major feature and there are a number of windows of the same period, as also is the font, with good carving and a pretty, later, cover. The roof is late-medieval and the robust pews date from about 1600. Restoration has been minimal.

Stone roofs and grey sandstone walls make this church seem as if it has grown from the ground on which it stands so stalwartly.

242 Whenby, St Martin
SE 631 699

Whenby is about seven miles east of Easingwold and ten miles north of York. It lies in undulating country and St Martin's stands on a bank above the road in a well-treed churchyard garnished in spring with snowdrops and daffodils.

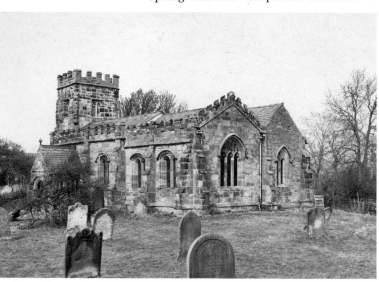

The present church is all Perpendicular but the masonry of the walls reveals that part of the building may be at least 200 years older. There was an extensive restoration in 1871 and further work in 1910. With their prominent battlements the nave, tower, chancel and porch present a distinctive appearance from all sides except the north where the humbly constructed north aisle shows a more austere profile.

Inside, the tower arch is offset to the north which probably indicates the remodelling of the 13th-century church in the 15th century. There is no chancel arch but the chancel screen is 15th-century and has traces of colouring. The screen to the north chapel is 17th-century and the door still has its original latch and hinges. In the nave are fourteen medieval benches.

A curious feature is the presence of a doorway in the east wall of the chancel, to the north of the altar – there is no evidence of a doorway outside.

243 York, Holy Trinity Goodramgate

W D Howells said it all in *Seven English Cities* (1909):

There is in York a little, old, old church whose dear and reverend name I have almost forgotten, if ever I knew it, but I think it is Holy Trinity, Goodramgate, which divides the heart of my adoration with the Minster.

It stands sequestered in a little leafy and grassy space of its own, with a wall hardly over-looked on one side by low stone cottages, the immemorial homes of rheumatism and influenza. The church had the air of not knowing that it is of Perpendicular and Decorated Gothic, with a square, high-shouldered tower, as it bulks up to a very humble height from the turf to the boughs overhead. The oaken pews are square and high-shouldered, like the low church tower, and, without, the soft yellow sandstone is crumbling away from the window traceries. The church did not look as if it felt itself a thousand years old, and perhaps it is not, but I never was in a place where I seemed so like a ghost of that antiquity. I had a sense of haunting it, in the inner twilight and the outer sunlight, where a tender wind was stirring the leaves of its embowering trees and scattering them on the graves of my 11th and 12th century contemporaries.

The floors and pews undulate like a swell at sea but the sandstone is not now crumbling as rapidly as it was eighty years ago.

Though there are traces of an older building, most of the structure we now see is of the 13th, 14th and 15th centuries. The marvellous stained glass in the east window was given by the Revd John Walker in 1470–1. There is also old stained glass in other windows. The furnishings date largely from the 17th and 18th centuries. There is much more – this is a church to explore.

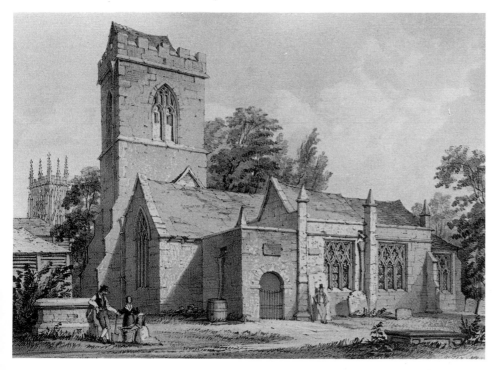

244 York, Old St Lawrence Walmgate Tower

All that remains of the medieval church which served the suburb just outside Walmgate along the Hull road, is this small tower. Behind it broods the grim late-19th-century church which replaced it. The tower is an essential part of the surviving medieval fabric of the city of York, and is enhanced by the addition of the fine Norman doorway of the Old Hospital Chapel of St Nicholas, carefully re-erected against it when that church was demolished in the last century.

Condition at the time of vesting.

SOUTH YORKSHIRE

245 Edlington, St Peter Old Church
SK 533 973

St Peter's is a late 12th-century church lying between Doncaster and Rotherham, consisting of nave, chancel, north aisle with chapel, west tower and south porch, dating from the period when the Norman style was becoming Transitional. It is a masterpiece of curious Norman carvings. The south wall retains its original corbel table and chevron; beak-head and other mouldings are used continuously to adorn the south door. The chancel arch has short responds starting on extremely high plinths and is decorated with several rows of chevrons. The upper storey of the tower is Perpendicular, as is the north chapel.

This was the first church to be vested in the Fund. It was unroofed by the diocese in 1966 and subject to constant vandalism. A demolition order for all but the tower was recommended at vesting. The steady local interest in this lovely building has justified the decisions of the Friends of Friendless Churches and the Fund to preserve it in its entirety.

246 Kirk Sandall, St Oswald
SE 609 081

St Oswald's Church in its spacious churchyard lies half a mile to the west of the present village. With the Don Navigational canal to the north, the Doncaster to Scunthorpe railway on one side and an industrial estate to the south, it is a setting made for Andrei Tarkovsky.

There is evidence of Saxon work in the west wall and south aisle and there are two Norman windows and a Norman doorway. The arcades are 13th-century, the west window dates from the early 14th and the chantry chapel for Archbishop Rokeby of Dublin (a former vicar) from the 16th. The Rokeby chapel (1520), with its fine monument to the Archbishop and memorials to other members of the family, and some interesting early-16th-century glass, is the special feature of the church.

The two screens which are now placed across the chancel arch and the arch at the east end of the north aisle probably

date from about 1520. They are exquisitively carved with traceried patterns incised with solid panels, forming a background to ogee arches and finials which are fixed on separately.

247 Throapham, St John
SK 523 876

St John's stands almost isolated at the southern end of a street that runs from Laughton-en-le-Morthen (with its splendid tower and spire) to Dinnington. There is a memorial slab to Robert and Alice Dinnington (d. 1432 and 1430) under the altar.

The south door is Norman and the main body of the church early-13th-century. The windows, clerestory and tower date from the 15th, as does the elaborately decorated font. The screen, now in the tower entrance, may be of similar date. The great treasure of the church is a beautifully carved coffin lid of c.1300. There are parts of memorial slabs set in the porch and a small Mauleverer brass of c.1620.

To the west is a medieval (or earlier) road which adds to the surprisingly strong sense of a really ancient past in this district, coexisting with modern artefacts that are rarely beautiful and at their worst in the churchyard of St John's, which is a *locus classicus* for degenerate funerary masonry.

248 Wentworth, Holy Trinity Old Church
SK 384 983

Replaced by Pearson's handsome new church in 1877, only a part of this building remains, but what does remain contains some of the Fund's best treasures. There is one wall of the ruined 1684 nave – the chancel and the 15th-century tower are nevertheless both roofed – and this provides an almost theatrical screen, a worthy contribution to an exceptionally picturesque village, close to both Rotherham and Sheffield.

The church's great glory is the series of memorials to the heads of the Wentworth family from 1548 to 1689, the most famous being Thomas, first Earl of Strafford, known as 'Black Tom Tyrant', and one of Charles I's closest advisers, whose head the Long Parliament demanded and obtained in 1641.

There are other monuments in the church and churchyard which illuminate local and national history, including a Gascoigne memorial (others are in the Fund's church at Harewood) and a 13th-century memorial of an archer. The stained glass, unusually, dates from the 1684 restoration by the second Earl of Strafford.

All is lovingly cared for and the church often houses exhibitions of some aspect of the local history of which it contains so much.

Late 19th-century photograph.

WEST YORKSHIRE

249 Harewood, All Saints
SE 314 451

Approaching Harewood House across the park, the church is hidden behind trees on the right. Built about 1410, various documents and stones nevertheless suggest a pre-Norman church on the site. Its Gothic was made Gothick, probably to John Carr's design, in 1793 and the Victorian restoration was by Sir George Gilbert Scott.

Internally, the building itself is severe. The columns have no capitals and there is little decorative carving. The greater therefore is the contrast with the six superb alabaster tombs dating from 1419 to 1510. They are virtually without rival in England, giving a history of how carving, funerary design and clothing developed during those years.

Two monuments commemorate Elizabeth and Sibilla, daughters of Lord Aldburgh, who built the church, and their husbands. A third is to Edward Redman, a 16th-century descendant of Elizabeth Aldburgh, who, despite his support for Richard III, was pardoned by Henry VII. The other three are Gascoignes (another is to be found at the Fund's church at Wentworth). Judge Sir William Gascoigne and Elizabeth Mowbray are the easternmost and oldest of the three. Above is an elegant monument to Judge Denison who wished to be commemorated near his illustrious predecessor.

A plaque records the burial there of Mary, the Princess Royal (d. 1965) daughter of George V and Queen Mary.

250 Leeds, St John the Evangelist
SE 302 338

St John's in Briggate was built in 1631 entirely at the expense of John Harrison, a noted merchant whose benefactions did much for a place that was already beginning to be important. Churches of this period are rare and this is one of the few Gothic buildings to be constructed in England a decade after Inigo Jones' work at Whitehall and Greenwich had announced a new age.

The fittings inside, particularly the screen, reflect Elizabethan and Jacobean taste and are probably by Francis Gunby, to whom is attributed much of the best woodwork of that date in and around Leeds. They also reflect conservative liturgical practice, a large area for preaching and the Word, then a screen through which communicants could draw near for the Sacrament.

Threats of demolition in the 19th century led to interventions, some a little severe, by Norman Shaw, Gilbert Scott and Temple Moore. The outcome richly rewards the visitor; this is a beautiful church, lovingly cared for, which is not just one of the major sights of Leeds but an important element in the jigsaw of the national architectural heritage.

Since 31 March 1989 the following churches have also been vested in the Fund:

AVON — BROCKLEY, ST NICHOLAS. Medieval church with stone pulpit of about 1480, gracefully remodelled in the 1820s from sketches by the rector, the Revd. Thomas Shrapnel Biddulph.

DERBYSHIRE — DERBY, ST WERBURGH, tower (1601–8) and old chancel (1689–90), which contains a superb iron font cover by Robert Bakewell. Here Dr Johnson married Tetty Porter in 1735.

ESSEX — LITTLE BROMLEY, ST MARY THE VIRGIN. Nave basically Norman, chancel c.1300, 15th-century tower and carved panels on the font ... and a sense of having grown out of its surroundings.

KENT — KINGSDOWN, ST CATHERINE. This is the Kingsdown near Sittingbourne. 1865 by E W Pugin, his only known Anglican church. A delightful period piece in an isolated setting.

NOTTINGHAMSHIRE — COTHAM, ST MICHAEL. The chancel and eastern end of the nave, with 1890 bell-cote, of a 14th-century church reduced in size in 1794, but with the old windows re-used.

SOMERSET — OTTERHAMPTON, ALL SAINTS. An unemphatic village church with a Norman font, 16th-century screen and other good fittings. Awful 1894 restoration.

SUFFOLK — STONHAM PARVA, ST MARY THE VIRGIN. 14th-century nave and chancel, handsome west tower, clerestory and south chapel all Perpendicular. The nave has a splendid double hammerbeam roof and there are many other interesting fittings.

WARWICKSHIRE — AVON DASSETT, ST JOHN THE BAPTIST. By Charles Buckeridge 1868–9, it is a handsome contributor, with its gold-coloured stone, to a glorious setting. It contains the effigy of Deacon Hugo, who died in 1240.

WEST YORKSHIRE — HALIFAX, ALL SOULS, HALEY HILL. 1856–9 by Gilbert Scott, who thought it his best church. A magnificent building and contents on a fitting site, rescued thanks to the vision of Marcus Binney.

Glossary

AISLE North or south extension to NAVE or CHANCEL, usually separated from them by ARCADES.

APSE A semi-circular or polygonal area at the eastern end of a church.

ARCADE A series of arches, supported by columns or pillars, either open or blind, i.e., closed with masonry.

ASHLAR Masonry consisting of squared and smooth stone for facing a rubble or brick wall.

AUMBREY A recess or small cupboard used for the safe-keeping of the chalice and other sacred vessels; usually found on the north side of the CHANCEL.

BAROQUE 17th- and 18th-century style, characterized by extravagant and curvaceous ornamentation.

BARREL VAULT Continuous arched roof.

BATTLEMENT An embattled parapet, cut with regular indentations or crenellations. Originally of defensive use, but mostly used on churches for decoration.

BAY A compartment into which the NAVE, CHANCEL or TRANSEPTS are divided; consisting of a section of each storey and marked off by the PIERS or pillars of the ARCADE.

BEAKHEAD An ornament found in carved NORMAN doorways, shaped like a grotesque bird or beast with its beak or tongue projecting downwards.

BELFRY The floor or stage in the church tower in which the bells are hung.

BENEFACTION BOARD Board listing the names of charitable benefactors, with their gifts or bequests.

BIER Movable stand on which the coffin is placed to carry it to and from the funeral service.

BOSSES Carved projections usually placed at the intersection of ribs of a vault.

BOX PEW An enclosed pew, entered by a door, usually large enough for one family.

BRACES Inclined timbers used in partitions and roofs which brace or tie together the main timbers.

BROACH SPIRE An octagonal spire springing from the square pyramidal top of a tower without a parapet.

BUTTRESS A projecting structure built against the outside wall giving it additional strength to resist the thrusts of arches, roof or vaults. A flying buttress does the same work by means of an arch or half-arch.

CAPITAL The head of a column or pillar, usually ornamented. A Corinthian capital is elaborately carved with acanthus leaves.

CARTOUCHE A tablet with an ornate frame, usually enclosing an inscription.

CHANCEL The eastern part of a church containing the high altar. It is often separated from the rest of the church by a screen.

CHANTRY-CHAPEL An endowed chapel, usually containing the tombs of the founder and family, and in which masses were said.

CHEVRON Zig-zag decorative moulding used in NORMAN architecture, especially around arches and doorways.

CLERESTORY Upper storey standing above the AISLE roof and pierced by windows.

COMMANDMENT BOARD See DECALOGUE.

CONSECRATION CROSSES Crosses painted on the wall to mark the places annointed by the bishop at the time of consecration, usually twelve in number.

CORBEL Stone block, usually moulded or carved, projecting from a wall and acting as a supporting bracket.

CORNICE The horizontal, moulded, projecting top edge of a building or pillar.

CRENELLATION See BATTLEMENT

CROCKET Small projecting sculpture in the form of foliage or flowers, used to embellish the angles of pinnacles, spires, gables and canopies.

CRESTING Continuous ornament, carved or pierced, surmounting a screen, canopy or CORNICE.

CROSSING   In cruciform churches, the part of the building where the NAVE, TRANSEPTS and CHANCEL meet.

CROW-STEPPED   The stepped, sloping edge of a gable.

CUPOLA   A small domed or polygonal turret crowning a roof.

CUSPS   Small projecting points with a foliated appearance on the curves of window and screen TRACERY, arches, panels, etc.

DADO   The lower part of an interior wall when specially faced or decorated.

DECALOGUE BOARD   Painted board hung in a church, on which the Commandments are written. Such boards became a regular feature of church furnishing in the reign of Elizabeth I.

DECORATED PERIOD   Phase of GOTHIC architecture in England prevalent from the late-13th to the mid-14th century. It is characterized by a greater use of decorative moulding and more elaborate window TRACERY than the EARLY ENGLISH PERIOD.

DIAPER WORK   The more or less complete covering of a wall surface with decorative patterns, often arranged in squares or diamonds.

DOG-TOOTH   Ornamentation in EARLY ENGLISH architecture resembling a square four-leaved flower, and thought to be based on the shape of the dogtooth violet.

EARLY ENGLISH PERIOD   13th-century phase of English GOTHIC architecture distinguished by its use of pointed arches and LANCET WINDOWS.

EASTER SEPULCHRE   A recess with a tomb-chest, usually in the north wall of the CHANCEL in which the host was ceremonially deposited from Good Friday to Easter Day.

ENCAUSTIC TILES   Process of decorating tiles and brick by burning-in different coloured clays to produce a stencil-like effect.

FAN VAULT   Vaulting of the PERPENDICULAR PERIOD in which the ribs of the ceiling form a fan-pattern angled in a trumpet-shape to a central point.

FINIAL   The curved or moulded ornament which terminates pinnacles, gables, etc.

FLUSHWORK   Wall decoration formed by an arrangement of knapped flints and brick or stone, often in a chequer pattern.

FOUR EVANGELISTS   Ss Matthew, Mark, Luke and John, often symbolized by, respectively, an angel, a lion, an ox and an eagle, and frequently depicted around the font.

FRIEZE   Band of decoration found along the middle part of the upper section of a wall.

GARGOYLE   A projecting spout, carved with grotesque features, designed to carry rainwater off the roof and away from the walls.

GOTHIC   Term applied to the architecture which flourished in western Europe from the 12th to the 16th century. The Gothic revival was a scholarly, Victorian rediscovery of the medieval style. Gothick is the name given to an 18th-century fashion based upon a fanciful interpretation of Gothic.

GRISAILLE   13th- and 14th-century stained glass having a greenish-grey hue.

HAGIOSCOPE See SQUINT.

HAMMERBEAM ROOF   A form of timber roof of late GOTHIC construction which avoids the use of a TIE-BEAM from wall to wall, the thrust being taken by two brackets, the upper and horizontal member of which is the hammerbeam. The ends of the beams are often decorated with carvings, especially with angels bearing shields.

HATCHMENT   Diamond-shaped boards bearing a coat of arms, which were carried in procession at the burial of the arms holder, then hung on the front of the house of the deceased and, finally, transferred to the church.

HOODMOULD   Projecting decorative ledge over heads of doors and windows to throw off rain-water; also called a dripstone or label.

IONIC PILLAR   Classical Greek form of pillar, of slender proportions with a fluted shaft and a CAPITAL decorated with volutes (spiral scrolls).

JESSE WINDOW   A window illustrating the genealogy of Christ in the form of a tree growing out of the body of Jesse, the father of David, through whose line Christ is descended; culminating in the Virgin Mary holding the Christ child.

KING-POST   Structural timber extending from the tie-beam of a roof-truss to the ridge. See also QUEEN-POSTS.

LABELSTOP The moulded or sculptured termination of a HOODMOULD or dripstone which runs over the top of an arch or window.

LADY CHAPEL Chapel dedicated to the Virgin Mary.

LANCET WINDOW Narrow pointed windows of the EARLY ENGLISH period named from its resemblance to a lance blade.

LATTEN A yellow alloy made from a mixture of copper and zinc identical to or resembling brass.

LECTERN Desk from which the Bible is read.

LIERNE Small connecting ribs creating an intricate pattern, used in 14th-century vaulting.

LINENFOLD Wooden ornamentation, carved to resemble the folds of linen, found in panelling of the TUDOR period.

LONG-AND-SHORT WORK QUOINS placed alternately horizontally and vertically at the corners of buildings. Characteristic of SAXON workmanship.

LUCARNE Small window in a spire.

LUNETTE Circular or semi-circular window or opening in a dome or vaulted ceiling to let in light.

LYCH-GATE A covered gateway at the entrance to a churchyard, under which mourners rested with the corpse before the burial service. From the Anglo-Saxon 'lich', a corpse.

MAIDENS' GARLANDS Garlands borne at the funeral of a virgin, and afterwards suspended in the church.

MEZZANINE Storey between two floors.

MISERICORD The lifting seat of a choir STALL, usually with a carved bracket on the underside and a smooth hollowed surface on the leading edge which gives some support to the occupant when standing during long services.

NARTHEX An enclosed area or porch at the western entrance to churches.

NAVE The main body of the church west of the CHANCEL, used by the congregation.

NICHE An alcove or recess in a wall for the display of a statue.

NORMAN ARCHITECTURE The English variant of ROMANESQUE, introduced by the Normans after 1066, with distinctive round arches and massive pillars.

OBELISK Tall tapering pillar.

OGEE A double-curved arch or moulding created by a concave and convex curve flowing one into the other.

ORATORY A chapel for private prayer.

PALL Linen cloth laid over the chalice at Eucharist, also a covering for the coffin or hearse.

PALLADIAN Architectural style introduced by Andrea Palladio (1508–80), based on ancient classical forms.

PARCLOSE A screen or railing separating a chapel or AISLE from the main body of the church or protecting a monument.

PARVISE An open space or porch at the entrance to a church or the room over the porch.

PATEN Small circular dish, usually of silver or pewter used to hold the Eucharist wafer.

PEDIMENT Triangular gable. A segmental pediment is a variation in which the triangle is replaced by a segment of a circle.

PERPENDICULAR The last phase of English GOTHIC architecture, flourishing from the late-14th to the 16th century, characterized by large windows, vertical lines of TRACERY, impressive towers and FAN VAULTING.

PETER'S PENCE BOX Box for collecting the annual tribute of one penny per household due to the see of Rome. Abolished in English churches by Henry VIII in 1534.

PEW RENTS Payment made by propertied families for the exclusive use of pews. Those nearest the altar attracting the highest rent.

PIERS A supporting structure from which arches or vaulting spring.

PILASTER Shallow column embedded in a wall.

PISCINA Recess with basin and drain for washing the sacred vessels.

POPPYHEADS Leaf-like FINIAL used to decorate the top of a bench-end. Poppy is thought to derive from 'puppis', meaning a ship's carved figure-head.

PRESBYTERY The eastern end of a church, the area east of the choir and including the altar.

QUATREFOILS Ornament in the form of a leaf or flower with four lobes.

QUEEN-POSTS Upright pairs of roof beams whose purpose, like the KING-POST, prevents sagging and adds stability.

QUOINS External angle stones.

REREDOS The wall or screen at the back of an altar, usually ornamented with painting, carving, statuary, etc.

RESPOND A half-pillar or pillar terminating an ARCADE.

RETICULATED Window TRACERY which developed during the DECORATED period, made up of circles which are elongated into OGEE shapes and repeated in a honeycomb pattern.

REVEALS The inward sloping jamb of a door or window, between the outside wall and the frame.

ROMANESQUE The style of European architecture prevalent from the 9th to the 12th century, perpetuating the round arch of the Romans.

ROOD A rood is a cross or crucifix, usually placed between the CHANCEL and the NAVE. The rood-beam carries the cross. The rood-screen separates the two parts of the church, and often has panels bearing a series of carved designs or painted figures. If the screen supports a gallery this is known as the rood-loft. The loft was reached by steps cut into the wall of the chancel or in a pillar, now often bricked up.

ROYAL PECULIAR A church not under the jurisdiction of the diocese in which it is situated, but under the personal authority of the Sovereign.

SADDLEBACK TOWER A tower with a pitched roof and gable ends.

SANCTUARY The most easterly and sacred part of the CHANCEL.

SAXON Pre-Conquest English architecture.

SCRATCH DIALS Simple sundials scratched into the stone near the south door or porch, used to tell the time for Mass.

SEDILIA Recessed seats in the south wall of the CHANCEL. Used by the celebrant and his assistants.

SOUNDING BOARD Structure placed over a pulpit to direct sound forwards, also called a tester.

SPANDREL The triangular space formed between two arches or between the exterior curve of an arch and the rectangular lines of a doorframe.

SPLAY Bevel or slope at a door or window, to increase illumination.

SQUINT Narrow oblique opening cut through the wall of a medieval church allowing the high altar to be seen from the AISLES, TRANSEPTS and side chapels. Also called a hagioscope.

STALLS Elaborate seating for the choir situated in the CHANCEL, often with canopies and carved MISERICORDS.

STOUP A basin, usually recessed in the wall near the main entrance, for holding holy water.

STRAPWORK 16th- and 17th-century decoration resembling straps.

STRING-COURSE A projecting, horizontal band of moulding running along the wall.

TESTER See SOUNDING BOARD.

THREE-DECKER PULPIT Pulpit with the clerk's stall and reading desk arranged in descending order.

TIE-BEAM A wall-to-wall cross-beam tied at its ends to the wall-plates.

TIERCERON Secondary rib springing to the ridge-rib of a vault.

TRACERY The ornamental stonework in the upper part of a window or filling in a circular window. Also used on tombs, screens, etc.

TRANSEPTS The projecting arms of a curciform church.

TRANSITIONAL A term generally used for the change from one architectural style to another, and in particular from the NORMAN to the GOTHIC periods.

TRIFORIUM An ARCADE above the arches of the NAVE and below the CLERESTORY.

TUDOR Last phase of the PERPENDICULAR style, in which the arch flattens out.

TYMPANUM The space between the lintel and arch of a doorway, or within a PEDIMENT.

WAGON ROOF A semi-cylindrical roof or vault.

ARCHITECTURAL PERIODS (approximate dates):

Saxon	7th c.	to	1066
Norman	1066	to	1145
Transitional	1145	to	1190
Early English	1190	to	1300
Decorated	1300	to	1350
Perpendicular	1350	to	1500
Tudor	1500	to	1603

Index

Printed in the United Kingdom for HMSO
Dd 291277   C50   3/90